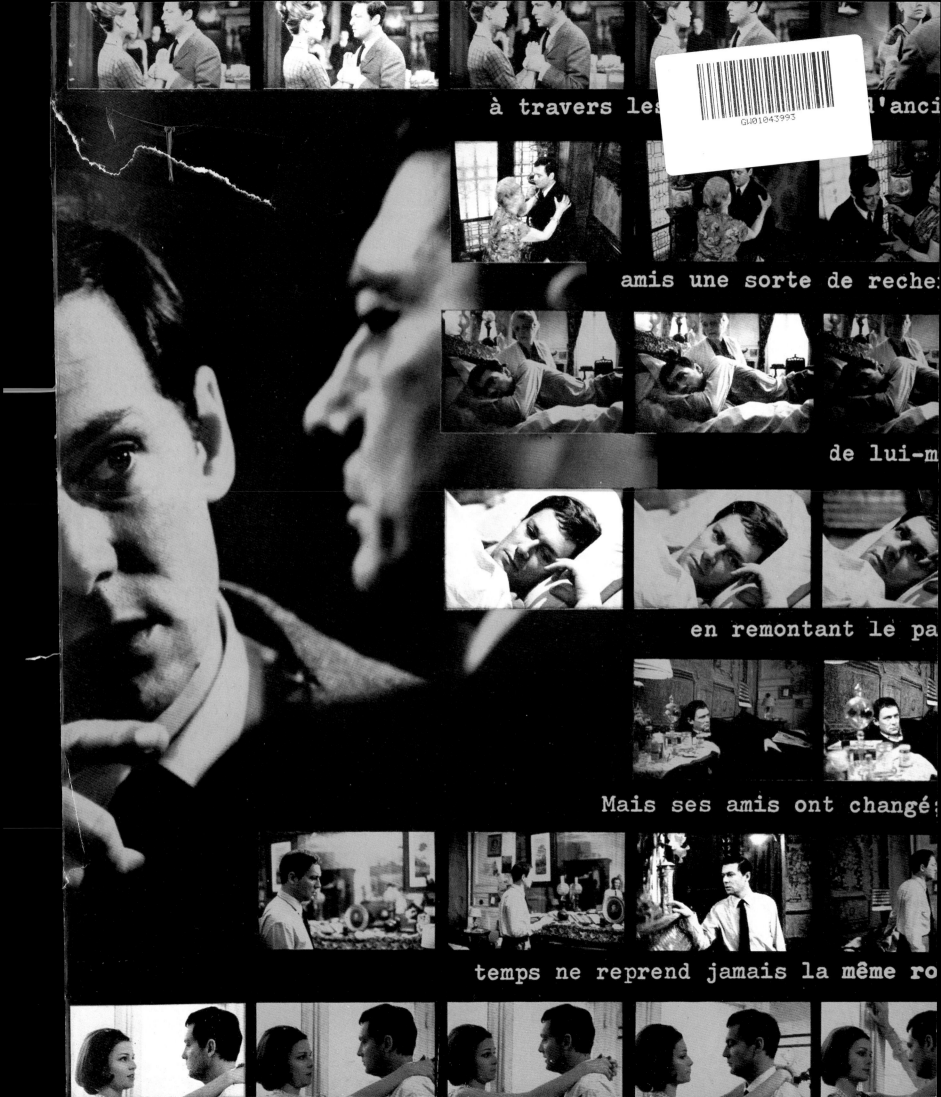

à travers les
d'anci

amis une sorte de reche

de lui-m

en remontant le pa

Mais ses amis ont changé

temps ne reprend jamais la même ro

Dieu a choisi Paris

french new wave

french new wave
a revolution in design

tony nourmand

graham marsh

christopher frayling

REEL ART PRESS

editor **tony nourmand**
art director **graham marsh**
introduction **christopher frayling**
text **alison elangasinghe**
deputy art director **jack cunningham**
editorial associate **rory bruton**

Hawks
par Jean A. Gili

néma d'aujourd'hui • Seghers

Vood

MOVIE PAPERBACKS

CAHIERS
DU CINÉMA

N° 1 • REVUE DU CINÉMA ET DU TÉLÉCINÉMA • AVRIL 1951

french new wave

a revolution in design

There's a sequence in François Truffaut's classic film about the making of a film, *Day for Night* (*La Nuit Américaine*) made in 1972, which says a lot about the contribution of the printed word to the 'new wave' which broke over French cinema from the late 1950s. In this sequence, the fictional director, M. Ferrand played by Truffaut himself, is facing a series of little crises on the set of the rather old-wave mainstream family melodrama he's trying to cobble together. His radical past is well behind him. One of the leading ladies is three months pregnant, another is having difficulty remembering her lines, there are budget difficulties, and the director has had a nightmare about what the critics will say: 'Why can't he make *political* films, like Jean-Luc Godard?' Suddenly, a messenger arrives, with a parcel of books ordered by the Truffaut character—and as the romantic theme music swells on the soundtrack—we see the director's hands, in close-up, opening the parcel. The books fill the screen, one piled on top of the other: *Alfred Hitchcock* by Robin Wood, *Howard Hawks* by Jean Gili, pamphlets about Ingmar Bergman, Luis Buñuel and Godard, a screenplay by Carl Theodor Dreyer . . .

The irony of the sequence lies in the evident contrast between the day-to-day problems of the film director—'like travelling in a Western stagecoach,' as he puts it, starting off optimistically then just struggling to do the best you can—and the romantic dreams of the auteur, the artist-hero who is in love with the cinema and wants his 'vision' to survive intact. He is an intellectual who evidently enjoys reading the latest critical studies of his favourite international directors, and who also enjoys the self-image of an 'author'—more than just a director-for-hire—but who finds himself constantly having to compromise with the inevitable realities of big-budget film-making.

Although its most significant contributions were to draw attention to a distinctive language of film—a visual language in its own right rather than a way of illustrating a literary or dramatic adaptation—and to the importance of the 'mise-en-scène', the director's personal approach to staging, the new wave always had a lot to do with print. First of all, there were the pioneering articles on 'film language' and 'the camera as pen' by André Bazin and Alexandre Astruc in the journal *La Revue du Cinéma* between 1946 and 1949. These laid the theoretical foundations for the new wave film-makers who made their presence felt some ten years later. Astruc wrote: 'The camera could become a means of writing as supple as subtle as written language and the cinema could truly make itself the expression of thought.'

Then there was the small group of critics-as-film-makers, film-makers-as-critics, those who thought of film-making as a form of criticism and vice-versa and who found an outlet for some of their energies on the magazine *Les Cahiers du Cinéma*, which succeeded *La Revue du Cinéma* onto the newsstands in April 1951. From the *Revue* (which died in 1949), *Cahiers* inherited both its editorial position: a concern with cinema as a means of capturing the essence of real-life experience, seen through the surface appearance of things—and its look: a distinctive mustard-yellow cover, with a large black-and-white press still and the title of the journal in bold, traditional typography. Like the cover of an exercise book.

One problem which the editors of the *Revue* had had was in getting to see the films, especially the American films which they passionately wanted to write about. It was no use rediscovering America in any systematic way, if the best the Champs-Élysées could offer was a few beaten-up, muddy prints of Laurel and Hardy shorts. The existence of two ciné-clubs in Paris which helped these would-be cinéastes catch up on the back numbers also had an important influence on the direction which the new wave was to take. There were others, but the first was the Cinémathèque, a fifty-seater co-founded and run by one of the world's great film obsessives, Henri Langlois, the man who was later to place Mom's mummified head from *Psycho*, a gift from Alfred Hitchcock, on his office desk (as I know from personal experience: it would stare at you balefully during attempts to interview Langlois); and the second was *Objectif 49*, a rather less down-to-earth club with Jean Cocteau, Robert Bresson and others on its committee, which tried to run a 'salon des refusés' in Biarritz, a film festival to rival—and criticise—Cannes; it folded after two years. Both the *Revue du Cinéma* and *Objectif 49* were more concerned with aesthetics than political ethics—or indeed with politics at all—and in particular they were concerned with the idea that a film was good to the degree that it expressed the author, the creator who had made it. And with the idea that film should be treated as the Seventh Art. This approach, too, was inherited by *Cahiers du Cinéma* in its early years. One of the many myths surrounding the journal is that its writers were all left-wing intellectuals who sought to challenge the political and cinematic status quo; there were one or two critics on the staff who had contributed to Communist periodicals in the late 1940s, but, on the whole, the early *Cahiers* people weren't interested in the sociology of the cinema and were mightily confused about debates about films and politics. They were less interested in themes and subjects beyond the screen than with *mise-en-scène*—what could be seen inside the frame. Many of them were centre-right. For example, when Sam Fuller's film *Pickup on South Street* was banned outright in France for its representation of the Communists as redder-than-red baddies, an article in *Cahiers* responded by saying that since Sam Fuller was an artist—a coarse artist, admittedly, rather than a fine artist—this shouldn't really matter. When others later drew attention to the racism in John Ford's Westerns, another article accused the accusers of 'provincial snobbery'. *Cahiers* did indeed issue a challenge to the cinematic status quo but, when it came, it was for very different apolitical reasons, and from a very different point of view. This challenge came in the second year of publication—in 1952/3—when a small but wild bunch of young men (and they were all men) who dreamed of becoming film-makers themselves started writing regularly for the journal. Some were making experimental short films at the same time. They were Jean-Luc Godard (under the pseudonym Hans Lucas), François Truffaut (sometimes under the pseudonym Robert Lachenay, which he seems to have pinched from the main character in Jean Renoir's *La Règle du jeu*, Robert de la Chesnaye), Maurice Scherer (under the pseudonym Eric Rohmer, a surname he took from the name 'Sax Rohmer', the author of the Fu Manchu stories and other Oriental mysteries), Jacques Rivette and Claude Chabrol. Most of the *Cahiers* brats, headed by Godard/Lucas, had met during 1950, while sitting in the front row of the Ciné-Club du Quartier Latin and writing for its bulletin, and while visiting the Cinémathèque. They liked to see *Cahiers* as their 'rancho notorious'—a hideout for cinematic outlaws, as in Fritz Lang's film: except that Lang's 'rancho' was run by a woman, and it took *Cahiers* over ten years to commission a single female critic.

In retrospect a legend has grown up around this group, which has it that they marched into the editor's office, took over the journal as a group and subsequently spoke, as it were, with one voice. Actually, it's clear from reading those early issues of *Cahiers* that, although they did share certain attitudes—as well as a preference for the front stalls, a burning ambition to make films, and, allied to that, a belief in a new canon of Hollywood film directors who understood cinema as a distinctive medium—they didn't, in fact, have many ideas in common. They certainly did not take over the journal, which remained very much André Bazin's territory until the late 1950s, with editorials criticising what they had to say and even the way they said it. While Jacques Rivette waxed lyrical about Howard Hawks as 'the only American director who knows how to draw a

moral', and Nicholas Ray was routinely compared with Beethoven, Bazin sometimes had to rein his young critics in, and remind them of the danger of 'an aesthetic personality cult'. They were on a 'hazardous adventure'—and they needed to be reminded that third-rate film-makers could have a vision of the world too. One thing they did agree about, on the subject of French films they all treated it as an article of faith that French cinema could and should become the very best in Europe: Italy had somehow stolen a march on them since the end of the war, some great films were coming out of Hollywood, especially those by misunderstood mavericks, and British cinema was scarcely worth writing about. If they became over-excited about some of their American or Italian or Japanese heroes, it was because they were *really* writing about what they hoped would happen in Paris.

What made them angry was the current state of *French* cinema, both the institution and the product: the '*cinéma de papa*'—daddy's cinema. They tended to have radical views about this *tradition de qualité*, where the films lacked an authentic or individual voice, where considerations of 'quality' overrode considerations of realism, where the studio photography was 'scholarly' and 'polished', where editing obeyed the rules and where the stories originated in heritage literature rather than on the streets. The publication on New Year's Day 1954 of 22-year-old François Truffaut's famous article on 'A Certain Tendency within the French cinema' in this sense marked a real moment of truth: in the article, Truffaut took apart a selection of mainstream French films which were going the rounds at the time, in the most aggressive language he could muster. They were the products of a 'closed world'. The 100th issue of *Cahiers* recalled how it was this which transformed the journal from being a diffuse collection of reviews, to becoming a publication with a cause: 'A leap had been made, a trial begun with which we were all in solidarity. Something bound us together. From then on, it was known that we were *for* Renoir, Rossellini, Hitchcock, and against X, Y and Z. From then on there was a doctrine, the *politique des auteurs*, even if it lacked flexibility . . . An "idea" had got under way which was going to make its obstinate way to its most logical conclusion: the passage of almost all those involved in it to directing films themselves.' One might add that the journal had been pulled together not so much by a theory or a critical position but by an ambition to make films, and *do* something about it. The six characters in search of an auteur didn't want to work in Hollywood, or at Cinecittà or at Pinewood—they wanted to work, on their own terms, in France. *Cahiers* is unique in avant-garde film criticism in its support for film as a career option. As Truffaut added: 'I do not believe in the peaceful coexistence of "the tradition of quality" and a cinema of auteurs.' What of the peaceful coexistence of 'a cinema of auteurs' and the French film industry? Would this new wave

Festival du film maudit (1949), French special sheet, art by Jean Cocteau

of necessity be restricted to short films and d-i-y features made on a shoestring budget? Surprisingly, no new wave films were awarded grants from the French government—under André Malraux's scheme of 'avances sur recettes'—before 1965. They depended, in the early years, on venture producers from outside the industry who were attracted by their energy and idealism.

Meanwhile, on the Left Bank, another group of ambitious film-makers, mostly not so young, was gathering—a group which included Chris Marker, Alain Resnais and Agnès Varda. They were more associated with *Cahiers*' arch-rival as a journal, the left-leaning *Positif*, and they had a more focused interest in documentary—especially the shifting boundaries between documentary and fiction—in left-wing political debate and in whether there could a filmic equivalent of the *Nouveau Roman*, the new novel. On the whole, they were more politically committed. It was *Positif* which was famously to attack la nouvelle vague in 1982 as 'very vague and not that new', and to criticise the *Cahiers* brats for confusing analysis of film with errant self-promotion. It was a *guerre de papier*.

The first coinage of the term 'Nouvelle Vague', in fact, came from *L'Express* newspaper in October 1957, as the title of a series of articles by journalist Françoise Giroud on the youth culture of the up-and-coming generation which had been born between the wars: originally, it had nothing to do with cinema. The first application to young film-makers came a year later, in the journal *Cinema '58*, the year Françoise Giroud published her book *The New Wave: Portrait of Today's Youth*. But the big moment—when the various groups of new film-makers and mavericks in France appeared publicly as a *group* for the first time—came at the Cannes Film Festival in 1959, the year during which an astonishing forty young French directors were given the chance to screen their own first films.

At Cannes that year, François Truffaut had been banned as a critic because he had been so very rude about the official French entries, but was warmly welcomed back as the director of *Les Quatre cents coups/ The 400 Blows*, which went on to win the Best Direction prize. As part of the Festival, seventeen new directors organised a high-profile seminar on everything that was wrong with mainstream French cinema, which was covered by *Arts* magazine. And a publicity photo was taken, on the steps of the Palais des Festivals. The group shot included François Truffaut, Jacques Rozier, Claude Chabrol, Jacques Doniol-Valcroze and—sitting at the back looking sideways in dark glasses, no doubt dreaming about how good it was to be making a feature film of his own rather than short ones— Jean-Luc Godard. It also included Roger Vadim, who had proved himself more interested in the waves of St Tropez and the naked body of Brigitte Bardot than in any other kind of wave, and Marcel Camus, who

won the Grand Prix that year with the rather old wave *Orfeu Negro/Black Orpheus* and who was 47 at the time. Plus several others who had or would have little to do with la nouvelle vague as generally understood. No matter, the new wave had been officially launched, with a bland press release of shared principles. As to whether there was any deeper consistency in the group, *Arts* magazine not surprisingly found 'un désaccord total sur le détail'. It was an understatement. A year later, Claude Chabrol was to tell *Le Monde* that the whole thing was probably a Gaullist plot to associate the regime running the 5th Republic with renewal and innovation—a kind of Gallic version of Cool Britannia in the 1990s.

So, in the construction of la nouvelle vague as the new intellectuals of the film world, as a brand almost, print played a key part. And there were not surprisingly countless references to print media in the films themselves. Iconic moments include Godard himself standing next to his female lead in a café reading a copy of *Arts* magazine with the Truffaut headline, 'Le Cinéma Français Crève Sous Les Fausses Légendes' (French cinema is imploding under its false legends), in the 1959 short *Tous les garçons s'appellent Patrick/All the Boys Are Called Patrick*; Jean-Paul Belmondo (as Michel Poiccard) posing beside a poster of Humphrey Bogart and imitating his mannerisms in *À bout de souffle/ Breathless* (1960); numerous textual interruptions—captions, handwritten poems, slogans, dedications, street advertisements—which were a key part of the new aesthetic; and, in *Day for Night* (1972, long after the wave had crested and the tide had gone out in France), the film director Ferrand as a young boy stealing a set of monochrome front-of-house stills from through a cinema's metal grille. And the new wave directors, like the fictional director M. Ferrand in *Day for Night*, did love books. They transposed the words 'author/auteur' and 'writing/écriture/cinécriture' from the world of literature to film. Some of them adored the melodrama of American policiers, by writers in the noir tradition such as Cornell Woolrich, Richard Stark, David Goodis, Ed McBain, Brett Halliday. In *The 400 Blows*, young Antoine Doinel (Jean-Pierre Léaud) lights a candle in his little bedroom shrine to Honoré de Balzac—Truffaut's favourite author. So although they were aiming for a distinctive cinematic language, the starting-point (however loosely defined) was often a work of literature.

During the 50th birthday celebrations of la nouvelle vague—half a century after that official moment of launch at Cannes—the very concept of a new wave was much debated. In the process of redefinition, the shorthand version much loved by some film history books—young director-writers who started out as critics using hand-held Cameflex cameras on the streets and in friends' apartments for low-budget films, casting fresh-faced friends of cast and crew who were good at improvisation and seemingly unaffected, recording direct sound, and in post-production inventing jump-cuts, collages, deliberately protracted takes and a new grammar of film as ways of challenging the moribund and sclerotic studio-based cinema of the older generation—all of this has taken quite a critical beating. Many of the young directors were not in fact their own writers, they were making short films before or during the time they wrote film criticism, several of the best-known actors (Jeanne Moreau and Jean-Paul Belmondo for starters) had been around for some time, and daddy's cinema turns out to have been much maligned, especially by the shrill and sometimes needlessly cruel François Truffaut. What of Bresson, Clouzot, Cocteau, Gance, Melville, Renoir and Rouch? What of the French avant-garde of the 1920s: L'Herbier, Clair, Delluc? Weren't some of the 'precursors' (as *Cahiers* called them) actually rather good? Just like the critical writings of some of them in *Cahiers* and *Positif*, the new wave was full of contradictions. As Truffaut said in October 1961, after all the excitement of Cannes had begun to die down: 'The New Wave was not a movement or a school or a group; it was a quantity.' A quantity which, whatever the latter-day critics may say in hindsight, did create some of the most memorable cinematic moments in film history. They include: the use of Miles Davis's smoky improvised trumpet music on the soundtrack of Louis Malle's thriller *Ascenseur pour l'échafaud/Lift to the Scaffold* (1958); Jeanne Moreau (as Jeanne) wandering around the garden of the Dijon mansion accompanied by the *andante* from Brahms's sextet No. 1 and filmed by Henri Decaë in *Les Amants/The Lovers* (1958); Antoine Doinel (Jean-Pierre Léaud) staring rebelliously at the camera—a zoom followed by a freeze-frame—with the sea behind him at the end of *Les Quatre cents coups/ The 400 Blows* (1959); Jean Seberg in her cropped hair selling the *New York Herald Tribune* as she walks down the Champs-Élysées in *À Bout de souffle/Breathless* (1959); the 11-year-old Zazie (Catherine Demongeot) in an orange sweater rushing around the closed Paris Métro stations in *Zazie dans le Métro/Zazie* (1960); the free-spirited Catherine (Jeanne Moreau) singing the song *Le Tourbillon/The Whirlwind* to her two friends Jules (Oskar Werner) and Jim (Henri Serre, on guitar) in *Jules et Jim/Jules and Jim* (1961); Odile (Anna Karina) dancing the Madison, with her partners in petty crime Arthur (Claude Brasseur) and Franz (Sami Frey), in a Paris café in *Bande à part/Band of Outsiders* (1964)—and their 9-minute 43-second dash around the Louvre; 'The Return', on a snowy Christmas Eve, as Geneviève (Catherine Deneuve) arrives at a garage in Cherbourg (where she grew up) in an expensive car, and Michel Legrand's main title theme swells on the soundtrack at the end of *Les Parapluies de Cherbourg/ The Umbrellas of Cherbourg* (1964); the crumpled Lemmy Caution (Eddie Constantine), in traditional Hollywood gumshoe outfit, arriving at the neon-lit hermetic city of Alphaville in *Alphaville* (1965); Ferdinand (Jean-Paul Belmondo) wrapping sticks of red and yellow dynamite around his blue-painted face, lighting the fuse and then changing his mind in *Pierrot le Fou/Pierrot Goes Wild* (1965). And many, many more. Of course, not all the films made by 'the quantity' were memorable or even significant. And there were new wave copyists who adopted newly fashionable techniques as a gimmick without fully understanding them in order to seem *à la mode*. But some of the films, and the moments, have richly deserved to enter the pantheon: they were to change the course of mainstream film history.

So, whatever the developments within the *haute culture* of critics, there's no doubt that, as a continuing inspiration to film-makers everywhere, and in its idiosyncratic way as a fundamental contribution to film criticism, the new wave was and is deeply significant. As Professor T. Jefferson Kline, a specialist in modern French culture, has written: 'It is the revolution in film practice that would eventually cause a concomitant sea change in writing about film that would, in turn, allow us to appreciate what was new in the "New Wave".' Part of that revolution was about sheer narrative energy and technical bravado—challenging the accepted ways of achieving things—which has had a deep influence on just about every national cinema you can think of: Western and Eastern European; Latin American; American; African.

Did that revolution extend to the graphic arts? The new wave owed much to print, but next to nothing has been written about the poster and publicity materials connected with the resulting films. More has been written about 'les affiches de papa'—such as Jean-Denis Malclé's poster for *La Belle et la Bête* (1946) based on Cocteau's fantastical style; or Cocteau's own calligraphic signature image of a face-as-harp in Mediterranean colours for *Le Testament d'Orphée* (1960). But did the new wave have the revolutionary effect on the printed image it was simultaneously having on the moving image—not just in France but throughout Europe? Did it embody a critique of the old ways of laying out posters? Did the director-critics' aesthetic admiration for some Hollywood auteurs extend to an admiration for the static images, the posters, which promoted their work? Or were the conventions of the mainstream Hollywood poster—the stars' faces prominently displayed, heightened dramatic moments taken from the film itself, type size made to conform to contractual stipulations, snazzy marketing slogans dreamt up by ad agencies, exclamation marks to heighten the ballyhoo—were these conventions to be questioned, like the visual grammar contained in papa's mainstream films? Would the new wave film-makers allow their poster designers more graphic freedom—no star pics, no photo-based scenes, typography integrated into the overall design, imagery as close to painting and printmaking and collage as to the requirements of corporate marketing departments? Or would they perhaps adopt a more minimalist approach—not attempting to distil the film's atmosphere, or to stage-manage the viewers' response in advance; not getting between the viewer and the film? Well, the answer—as with so many aspects of the new wave—is in some ways they did and in some ways they didn't. All the above and none of the above.

European posters for Hollywood films had been evolving their own distinctive styles for a very long time, as Hollywood studios set up alliances with European distributors. Some of these posters had given more prominence to the director over the star, and had made little attempt to mimic the visual style of the films themselves. Peter Strausfeld's woodblock and linocut images made specially for the Academy Cinema on London's Oxford Street from 1951 onwards are excellent examples. One of the most infamous local variations was Anselmo Ballester's 1954 watercolour poster for *On The Waterfront*, which had a grim, gun-toting Marlon Brando striding towards the viewer—looking as though he was about to have a shootout with gangsters rather than a confrontation with union bosses!

By the late 1950s, various tendencies in graphic design—among them photography taking over from illustration, with hybrids becoming very fashionable; pared-down imagery taking over from clutter; text becoming part of the visual image and vice-versa, so together they worked overall as graphic design; photo-montage, collage and cut-ups; customised typography; torn-edges to the paper; graphic imagery learning lessons from post-war fine art—were already happening, and some new wave posters took full advantage of them. Images—like the moving images they were promoting—appeared in a wide range of styles and formats. Think of Clément Hurel's disturbingly cropped photomontage of a kissing couple against a black background with a slit of white, used to advertise *À bout de souffle/Breathless*. And compare it with the slightly old-fashioned glamour poster of Brigitte Bardot—come hither eyes, pouting lips, long dishevelled hair, prominent cleavage—designed by Georges Allard for Godard's *Le Mépris/Contempt* of three years later; or with the various attempts by designers to make Bardot and Anouk Aimée (as Lola) look more undressed than they were in the films. Or with Christian Broutin's iconic poster for *Jules et Jim* (1961), an image of a laughing Jeanne Moreau which combines photography (the face) with illustration (the coat and hair), with a white aura around both, on a green background, that seems to be sexy and dangerous in equal measure—just like the character she plays in the film. Or with Jean-Michel Folon's blue-and-black minimalist poster—of a film-noir cat with Eiffel Towers for eyes—for *Paris vu par . . ./Six in Paris* (1964). So, a wide range—much of it using the new graphic language.

At their best—some of the young French graphic designers; several of their Polish, Czech, Hungarian, Romanian, West and East German, and Japanese counterparts—these posters did amount to a revolution in design, just as some of the films amounted to a revolution in film. The energy of the films somehow influenced the graphic energy of the posters. There were experiments with typography—Jean Mascii's *Alphaville* written in neon; Hans Hillman's *Week-end* with the middle letters of the title out of focus, displayed diagonally across a dark background, as if on a car's windscreen; Clément Hurel's style B poster for *À bout de Souffle/Breathless*, with the A, B, D and S foregrounded and Jean Seberg's face looking quizzically at the result. There were collages—René Ferracci's *Deux ou trois choses que je sais d'elle/Two or Three Things I Know About Her*, with Marina Vlady's face surrounded by stills, advertisements and faces; Jaroslav Fišer's *Cléo de 5 à 7/Cleo from 5 to 7*, a graphic of her elongated face with playing cards falling below—symbolising her anxiety about the doctor's diagnosis. There were cut-ups: Hans Hillman's *Muriel*, a photo of a woman's lips revealed through torn pieces of paper, the credits in handwriting below; Waldemar Świerzy's *Les Quatre cents coups/The 400 Blows*, with a painting of Jean-Pierre Léaud's face cut into strips. There were visual symbols of the entire film rather than any images from the film itself, graphic representations of the main theme of the narrative as interpreted by the designer—Jacek Neugebauer's *Au Hasard Balthazar/Balthazar*, showing a tiny donkey with a huge burden on its back (the credits printed on it), brown on beige; artistic duo Jouineau Bourduge's *Le Trou/The Hole*, with six mug-shots of prisoners plus their reference numbers, the director's name in large letters the rest tiny, and a tunnel-hole through the letter 'o'; Carlantonio Longi's *Les Amants/The Lovers*, featuring two hands on a bed, the hands of the impetuous lovers Bernard and Jeanne-Bernard's on top—as if already aware of the film's controversial reputation. And caricatures—such as Pierre Étaix's elongated drawing with thick black border of Jacques Tati for *Mon Oncle/My Uncle*, plus little boy and dog, accompanied by minimal information beyond the director's name, an image which seems to be in dialogue with André François's cut-out, raising his hat, for Etaix's own *Le Soupirant/The Suitor*, complete with bullet-holes and a rifle target which have little to do with the charming comedy it was promoting. Even press-books, famously dull in layout as a rule, were sometimes jazzed up. Most American posters for new wave films, assuming them to be of niche interest, were covered in credits and press quotes, as if they were promoting newly-published books. Exceptions included Everett Aison's one-sheet for *Zazie dans le Métro/Zazie*, which turned the title into the Eiffel Tower, with lettering in red, white and blue; Milton Glaser's Munch-like image for *La Guerre est finie/The War is Over*, printed for a New York

screening; and the Pop Art *Mister Freedom*, showing a hunky superhero in an American football outfit, clutching a femme fatale dressed as a drum majorette, like a pop version of *King Kong* or *Robby the Robot*. Even the more mainstream European posters for new wave films have a freshness about them, especially the painted ones. A bit like M. Ferrand's hard-won film within a film in *La Nuit Américaine/Day for Night*. Or like the double-sided posters published by the West German distributors Constantin, which featured a traditional design on one side, an arty one on the other: cinema managers could choose which design suited the local clientele. Oddly, Italian posters for French New Wave films—usually sticking to the 'watercolour' tradition—tended to look more conventional than the equivalent posters of Italian, home-grown, films. It may be significant that Jackson Pollock's action paintings reached Paris in 1959, and Mark Rothko's in 1962—just at the time when some new wave film-makers were at their most confident in challenging the old-fashioned figuration that papa liked so much. Some of the European posters were so abstract as to lose all contact with the films they were marketing—such as Czech and Polish images for *Hiroshima, mon amour/Hiroshima My Love*, and a Zdeněk Kaplan design for *Le Petit Soldat/The Little Soldier* which resembles Francis Bacon's figures at the base of the crucifixion only in black and white this time, with a splash of red.

This book is a compendium of posters for French new wave films, with accompanying still images and press-books. It is organised around the designers (at last!), listed A-Z, rather than around the more usual film titles or national styles. It emphasises the key contribution of Eastern European designers as well as Western Europeans—and Japanese designers as well. It shows, among many other things, how far national campaigns differed from one another some sixty years ago which makes it a timely volume, when movie posters these days tend to be part of bland, global digital marketing campaigns, with graphic devices which are re-usable in a variety of formats; when distinctive poster identity is becoming an endangered species.

French New Wave: A Revolution in Design has been assembled with their characteristic flair and style by Tony Nourmand and the team at Reel Art Press. You've seen the films and DVDs and downloads. Now's the chance to relate them to the publicity in a book which is certainly new and not at all vague.

Christopher Frayling
May 2019

paris blues

scoring for the new wave

In Le Poste Parisien recording studios on the night of 4 December 1957, Miles Davis stood in a darkened room in front of a screen onto which jazz-loving, French New Wave film director Louis Malle projected scenes from his debut movie. While the star of the film, Jeanne Moreau, mixed the drinks, Davis and solid expatriate drummer Kenny Clarke, plus three French musicians—tenor saxophonist Barney Wilen, pianist René Urtreger and bassist Pierre Michelot—improvised the score as the images played out on the screen. They nailed it in a single session. The black and white film was a thriller starring Jeanne Moreau, Maurice Ronet and Lino Ventura called *Ascenseur pour l'échafaud/Lift to the Scaffold*. For Louis Malle and Miles Davis it was a transatlantic meeting of minds, which resulted in the most hauntingly beautiful soundtrack ever produced for any of the French New Wave films, indeed possibly in all cinema. It was the first encounter between black American modern jazz and the New Wave—so cool it was sub-zero.

Davis was no stranger to Paris, he had lived at the Hotel La Louisiane at 60 Rue de Seine in the Bohemian area of Saint-Germain-des-Prés, where he rubbed shoulders with some of the great artists in the city such as Jean Cocteau, Picasso and scene-maker and polymath Boris Vian. Saint-Germain-des-Prés was without a doubt the artistic and cultural hub of Europe immediately following the Second World War. Indeed, Vian was one of the magnets that drew American jazz musicians to Paris—he was known for his superb taste in jazz, admiration of beautiful women (who admired him right back) and an appreciation of the sweet life. Davis went to all the hip clubs and cafés around Saint Germain with the renowned writer and existentialist Jean-Paul Sartre and in the midst of all this social whirl, fell in love with French torch singer and actress, Juliette Gréco. The Left Bank of Paris in the 1950s was undoubtedly existentialist central. The jazz was modern, the movies were cool and the clothes were predominantly Ivy League. These were just some of the American influences that many of the French New Wave directors like François Truffaut, Jean-Luc Godard and Jean-Pierre Melville loved in equal measure. It was no surprise then, that after the success of Davis's score for *Lift to the Scaffold*, respected American and home-grown French musicians produced soundtracks that were Modern Jazz influenced. For many of the talented black musicians working in Paris this meant greater creative freedom and social acceptance, as well as providing a regular pay cheque.

Paris as a quintessentially hip location was a given but another strong visual influence—particularly on the New Wave film posters—were the graphic black and white photographs used on the covers of imported American modern jazz albums. One classic was Dexter Gordon's 1963 Blue Note album *Our Man in Paris*. Gordon is wearing a rounded (club) collar shirt with a collar pin. He also has the obligatory cigarette in his hand and the type reflects the colours of the French flag. Coincidentally, the French musician Pierre Michelot, who played bass on *Lift to the Scaffold*, plays on Dexter's album.

In Paris during the early 1950s to the late 1960s the roll call of outstanding American jazz musicians read like a sharply dressed register of the finest instrumentalists: Dizzy Gillespie, Thelonious Monk, Art Blakey, Stan Getz, Dexter Gordon to name but a few, all played the numerous clubs the City of Light had to offer and in-between gigs laid down tracks to accompany the New Wave celluloid. The collective music for the French New Wave cut through the old school like fresh battery acid.

The French composers and musicians were no slouches as their soundtracks testify. *À bout de souffle/Breathless* (1959), directed by Jean-Luc Godard, had an achingly hip minimalist score by Martial Solal, who also provided the music to *Deux hommes dans Manhattan/Two Men in Manhattan* (1959), directed by Jean-Pierre Melville. Michel Legrand composed the lush, memorable music for *Les Parapluies de Cherbourg /The Umbrellas of Cherbourg* (1964) directed by Jacques Demy, and Frances Lai provided the ultra-romantic score for *Un Homme et une femme/A Man and a Woman* (1966) directed by Claude Lelouch. These were composers at the top of their game.

The fashionable and the aware audiences worldwide embraced the French New Wave films and all their manifestations. The mannerisms and attitudes of the leading French actors—Jean-Paul Belmondo, Jean-Louis Trintignant and Alain Delon plus Brigitte Bardot, Jean Moreau and Jean Seberg—were much copied by knowing modernist faces from London to Tokyo. It was a movable feast of corduroy jackets, penny loafers, trench coats, Breton T-shirts and capri pants. Indeed, in many pockets a navy-blue beret nestled alongside a pack of Gitanes.

The French New Wave lasted just over a decade but the influences of those years, between 1958 and 1969, was immense and can still be seen and heard today. Contemporary movies and the design world owe a large debt to the New Wave movement which has been much copied—but never bettered. Even the American director Quentin Tarantino named his film company A Band Apart, after the 1964 Jean-Luc Godard film.

Graham Marsh
July 2019

à
bout
de
souffle

la nouvelle pop

there were no rules

When I began dealing in vintage movie posters 30 years ago, I was very much aware of the poster art of the French New Wave. At this time, and many years before I had Reel Art Press, I used to edit books on movie posters for other publishers. I was offered a book on a collection of French New Wave posters by a friend and collector, Serge Zreik. My publisher at the time wasn't interested, however, Serge's collection ignited in me a deeper interest in the French New Wave and my eyes were opened to a movement that had happened but had not been properly documented. I spent the next 20 years building what is now the largest collection of French New Wave advertising material in the world, with posters from over 20 countries and containing over 3000 items, including photographs, press-books, magazines and more. I am very happy that the current owner has allowed me to carry on expanding the Collection and to make this book possible.

The French New Wave is one of the most influential movements in the history of cinema. Its associated poster art also stands as one of the most influential design movements in the history of movie advertising. When looked at as a body of work, it vibrates with a restless and modern energy. Explosive and groundbreaking, the posters were a revolution in design.

Pop Art was a movement that arose in the 1950s and 1960s as a rebellion against an elite and pretentious art world. Instead, it took its inspirations from cinema, Americana and the everyday. Likewise, the French New Wave movement was a rebellion against the past. It broke with the establishment. It took its inspirations from cinema, Americana and the everyday. The way that narrative and images were presented was turned on its head. The same was true of the poster art. The artists tasked with selling the films of the New Wave to a global audience—from Poland to France to Japan—broke with the establishment and wrote their own script.

When rules are broken in any medium, it is only a success if the people breaking the rules understand their subject matter. The directors of the French New Wave were cinephiles, with an encyclopedic knowledge of film. The vast majority of poster artists working on campaigns for these films had gone to art school and were fluent in more traditional disciplines. So when it came to subverting conventions—subtly, playfully or aggressively—they did so with flair, fusing a technical proficiency in painting and illustration with new trends in photomontage, comic and Pop Art. The poster artists of the New Wave were the first to introduce these movements to the masses, taking Pop Art out of uptown galleries for the first time to the everyman on the street. Posters like Clément Hurel's *À bout de souffle* or René Ferracci's *Deux ou trois choses que je sais d'elle* are as important as some of the most famous Pop Art collages from the time.

The revolution in poster design that happened with the French New Wave did not happen in a vacuum. Poster design had gone through distinct phases in the twentieth century. In the 1920s and 1930s, movie posters were influenced by Art Deco and Art Nouveau. In the 1940s, there was no unifying theme in design, except for specific genres—for example film noir posters were very colourful despite the films themselves being very stark. The Second World War brought paper and ink shortages and had a stultifying impact on look and design. From the 1950s, there was the first evidence of experimentation and a more graphic-design approach to the marketing of films. In America, innovative designers like Saul Bass and Paul Rand were beginning to use symbols and graphic elements to sell movies—even if the purity of their creations was then diluted by the studio arbitrarily adding still photographs onto their designs. Bass and Rand were also singular examples in a still overwhelmingly traditional industry. In Eastern Europe from the mid-1950s, state-controlled film distribution had the effect of freeing poster artists from capitalist obligations to market big stars for big money and there was a resultant flood of creative freedom. This school of Eastern European poster design embraced pared-down graphics, abstraction, surrealism, humour and was fiercely experimental. From the late 1950s in France, poster artists were embracing photomontage and a less fussy approach to marketing. In Japan, the increasing interest in arthouse cinema led to a flowering of creativity among young poster designers—even renowned graphic designer Kiyoshi Awazu turned his hand to film posters. In Italy the posters remained painterly with a classic focus on portraiture, however, there was a bolder and more imaginative approach to design and colour. Globally, poster artists were experimenting and pushing the boundaries of representation. The outpouring of creativity was fueled by the cultural, political and civil upheavals of the 1960s and the wave was unstoppable.

Poster artists, however, were still beholden to the more orthodox demands of the studios, who had strict requirements for the treatment of stars and subject matter. Part of the reason that the poster campaigns for the New Wave were allowed to be so bold was that the films were often given a more limited global release, distributed by smaller, independent companies who had a greater appreciation for the poster as artform. Or if the films *were* distributed by one of the big studios, they were more prepared to take a risk with an arthouse title than one of their blockbuster hits. The result was that as a body of work, as a movement, the poster art of the French New Wave is unique in embodying the energy, freshness and power of that time.

When I started doing books on movie posters all those years ago, I always enjoyed unearthing new information on the poster artists. One of the most pleasing aspects of working on this book has been giving space to comprehensive artist biographies, making this the foundation of the book's structure. It has not always been an easy task to track down information—for too long, poster artists have been overlooked as a group, given too little credit for the relevance of their work, and there is a dearth of source material out there. It is a relief to finally give weight to the authors of such groundbreaking and original work.

Tony Nourmand
September 2019

Ascenseur
pour
l'échafaud

la porte s'ouvre sur
un cinéma nouveau

PIERRE BRAUNBERGER
présente

PRIX LOUIS DELLUC
1958

moi,
un
noir

«treichville»

un film en couleur
de
JEAN ROUCH

JEAN PAUL
BELMONDO

LO
SPIONE

*Charles
Aznavour

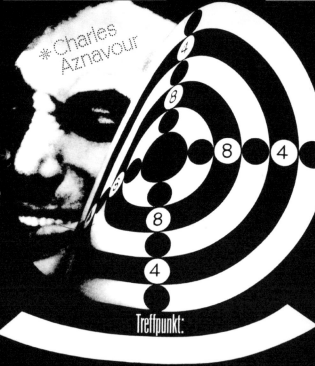

Treffpunkt:

ZAZIE
DANS
LE MÉTR

ФРАНЦУЗСКИЙ ХУДОЖЕСТВЕННЫЙ ФИЛЬМ
Режиссёр ФРАНСУА ТРЮФФО
ЧЕТЫРЕСТА УДАРОВ

Qui êtes-vous Polly Maggoo ?

UN FILM DE
WILLIAM KLEIN

DOROTHY MAC GOWAN
JEAN ROCHEFORT
SAMI FREY
GRAYSON HALL
AVEC LA PARTICIPATION DE
PHILIPPE NOIRET
ET ALICE SAPRITCH
DELPIRE PRODUCTIONS

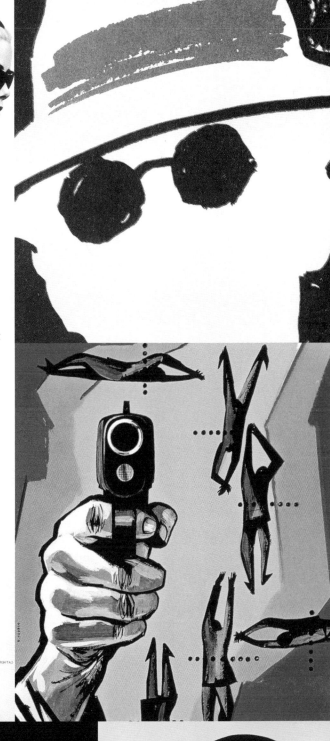

...ture"
rix Du
Francais

DIS TRUFFAUT "STOLEN KISSES"

アンリ・ダルクの発禁の書に挑んで
大胆に女体の神秘をえぐり出した
巨匠ルイス・ブニュエルの問題作！

昼顔

カラー作品

昭和44年度芸術祭参加作品

カトリーヌ・ドヌーヴ　ジャン・ソレル
ミシェル・ピッコリ＝主演
監督＝ルイス・ブニュエル
原作＝ジョセフ・ケッセル　フランス・東和の提携作品
製作・三船和照版

AWOT
東和提供

UDDENLY THE WORD
S ALPHAVILLE...
d a Secret Agent is in a
eathless Race Against

artists a–z

HITLER...
connais pas

Un film de BERTRAND BLIER
Produit par ANDRÉ MICHELIN

aage martin lundvald

(1908 Copenhagen, Denmark—1983)

Aage Martin Lundvald was one of the most well-known Danish poster designers of the twentieth century, responsible for hundreds of film campaigns. He frequently focused on the female protagonist, portraying her in stylised, cartoonish form with clean lines. His work was infused with a lightness and wit—a joyful enticement to audiences.

After briefly flirting with studying law, Lundvald pursued a career in art from his late teens, securing his first commission at the age of just 19 from Wilhelm Hansen, the prestigious music publishing house. He went on to work on strip cartoons and magazine illustrations, book covers and occasionally music composition. In 1937 he produced his first film poster, *Life at Hegnsgaard*. Movie posters became his main focus from this point onwards for both Danish and foreign releases. His early work is characterised by photography and a more traditional approach to film promotion, however, from the 1950s, he was given greater freedom to develop his own distinctive style.

Le Mépris (1963), Danish one sheet

-hendes navn betød kærlighed.

JACQUES DEMY's
fascinerende franske storfilm med
ANOUK
AIMÉE
MARC
MICHEL
ELINA
LABOURDETTE

ALAN SCOTT · JACQUES HARDEN
MARGO LION

PRODUKTION:
CARLO PONTI · GEORGES DE BEAUREGARD

UDLEJNING: A/S ASA FILMUDLEJNING

Lola (1961), Danish one sheet

LOPOTT CSÓKOK

A "NÉGYSZÁZ CSAPÁS" ANTOINE-JA A FELNŐTTKOR KÜSZÖBÉN

SZÍNES FRANCIA FILM   16 ÉVEN FELÜLIEKNEK

Baisers volés (1968), Hungarian one sheet

Les Parapluies de Cherbourg (1964), Hungarian one sheet

andrzej krajewski

(1933 Poland—2018 Newark, New Jersey, USA)

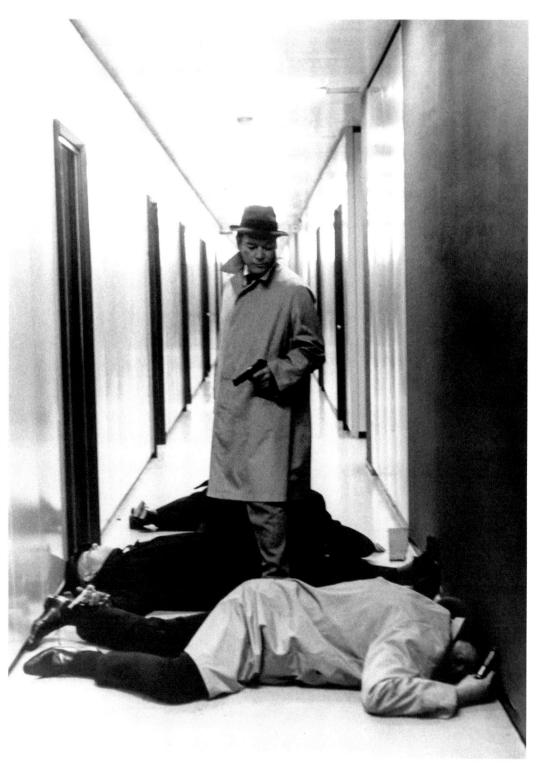

As a mass medium in Poland, the poster was under state censorship yet the individual artist had a remarkable degree of creative freedom. The poster as artform flourished in Poland from the mid 1950s onwards. Free of capitalist constraints, images of the stars—usually a big selling point in the West—were subordinated to highly original concepts. This 'Polish poster school' of artists that emerged effectively turned the street into their own gallery. Designs were striking and colourful; often disturbing and surreal; frequently poetic and humorous, with a vitality in stark contrast to the turgid backdrop of the Eastern Bloc. Some of the foremost representatives of the Polish poster school include Jan Lenica, Waldemar Świerzy and Franciszek Starowieyski. Many of these artists had studied under the 'father' of the Polish school, Henryk Tomaszewski, in his Department of Graphic Arts and Posters at the Warsaw Academy of Fine Arts. The Polish school's influence on the development of graphic design and visual culture worldwide has been huge and lasting.

Andrzej Krajewski (Andre de Krayewski in America) was a painter, illustrator, comic and collage artist with a career spanning over 60 years. He was an innovator of the Polish school who studied under Tomaszewski. Krajewski favoured bold Pop Art designs—the poster for Godard's dystopian sci-fi thriller *Alphaville* an example of his approach. Krajewski designed several film, theatre and political posters in Poland until 1985 when he emigrated to the States. In 1997 he was the official artist for the Panasonic Jazz Festival and he painted a famous New York Film Academy poster that was used around the country for many years. In the late 2000s, he wrote a novel about trying to escape from behind the Iron Curtain in the early 1950s.

Le Soupirant (1962), French one sheet

andrzej onegin-dabrowski

(1934 Radom, Poland—1986)

Agnès Varda was a visionary pioneer in cinema. Often called the mother or grandmother of the French New Wave, Varda was a rare female voice in the movement. She was hugely influential and her work is venerated today.

Cléo de 5 à 7 was Varda's second feature and was a real-time 90-minute portrayal of a young singer (played by Corinne Marchand) as she awaits the results of a possible cancer diagnosis. The film reflects on many themes but central is an existential look at mortality. Polish artist Andrzej Onegin-Dabrowski's poster for the film captures this perfectly, with Cleo seen fading away into suggested death.

Dabrowski was an award-winning Polish poster designer who had studied under Henryk Tomaszewski at the Warsaw Academy of Fine Arts. He created a number of celebrated film posters including Antonioni's *L'Eclisse* (1962) and Coppola's *You're a Big Boy Now* (1966).

DRAMAT PSYCHOLO-
GICZNY PRODUKCJI
FRANCUSKO-WLOSKIEJ
CLEO OD 5-ej DO 7-ej
REŻYSERIA: AGNES VARDA
W ROLACH GŁÓWNYCH:
CORINNE MARCHAND,
MICHEL LEGRAND, DOROTHÉE
BLANK, ANTOINE BOURSEILLER,
JOSÉ-LUIS DE VILALLONGA
PRODUKCJA: ◆ R O M E -
PARIS-FILMS ◆
◆ ◆ ◆ ◆

Cléo de 5 à 7 (1962), Polish one sheet

angelo cesselon

(1922 Cinto Caomaggiore, Italy—1992 Velletri, Italy)

Godard's exuberant and playful homage to American crime movies, *Made in USA*, was an assault of colour and Pop Art madness. Artist Angelo Cesselon was a fitting choice to illustrate the Italian poster as he was a master of colour, renowned for his vibrant palette. Cesselon worked with the most up-to-date oil paints on the market to produce the brightest colours possible, even changing Anna Karina's yellow dress to a vivid hot pink. He worked with fast brush strokes and often used white space around his images to emphasise movement and gesture, as seen here with Karina's leg and shooting arm. Cesselon was celebrated for his talent as a portraitist and for being able to choose the most appropriate 'key image' to promote a film. In 1955 he won the Italian Spiga Cambellotti prize as best cinematographic painter of the year. His most renowned posters include the classic Italian neo-realist films *Stromboli* (1950) and *Umberto D.* (1952).

Made in USA (1966), Italian four sheet

anna huskowska

(1922 Czernięcin, Poland — 1989 Warsaw, Poland)

A reworking of the ancient Greek myth of Orpheus and Eurydice, Marcel Camus' *Orfeu Negro* transported the fated lovers to the frenzy of modern-day Rio de Janeiro during *Carnaval*. A blaze of vivid colour, dance and beautiful sequences, the film features an almost all-black cast and won the Cannes Film Festival's Palme d'Or and the Academy Award for best foreign-language film. Perhaps its biggest cultural impact was the lush soundtrack (composed by Luiz Bonfá, João Gilberto and Antônio Carlos Jobim), which introduced the *bossa nova* style to an audience outside of Brazil for the first time and became hugely popular worldwide throughout the 1960s.

Anna Huskowska had studied at the Warsaw Academy of Fine Arts under Henryk Tomaszewski, graduating in 1956. She was a painter, exhibition designer and author of satirical drawings. She created a number of film and work safety posters, often favouring bright colours and bold brush strokes.

Orfeu Negro (1959), Polish one sheet

árpád darvas

(1927 Hungary—2015)

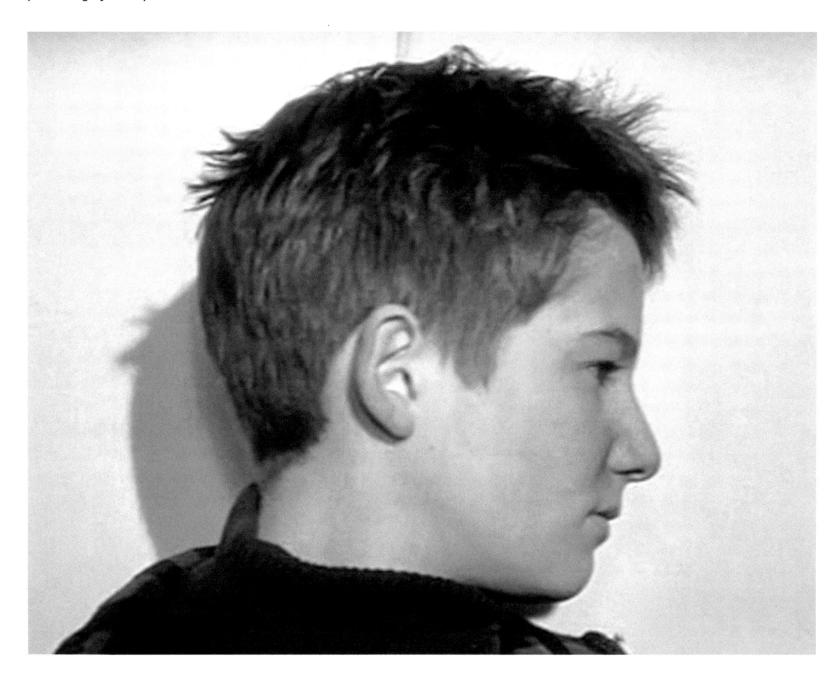

Alongside contemporaries like András Máté, Árpád Darvas pioneered a new approach to poster art in the country from the 1950s onwards. Hugely influential, he worked in many styles—painting, photomontage, surrealism, comic and Pop Art, among others—employing an expressive use of colour across these approaches.

After studying at the University of Applied Arts and University of Fine Arts in Budapest, Darvas began work as a poster artist for MOKÉP, the biggest film distribution company in Hungary. His large body of work includes posters for *8½* (1963), *My Fair Lady* (1964) and *The Battle of Algiers* (1966). In 1964, Darvas received the country's Mihály Munkácsy Prize, given to artists of exceptional talent, and in 1970 and 1975 he won awards for Best Poster of the Year. From 1963 to 1982, Darvas was a member of the Papp Group and from 2004, he was a member of the Hungarian Poster Association.

Les Quatre cents coups (1959), Hungarian one sheet

averardo ciriello

(1918 Milan, Italy—2016 Rome, Italy)

In Italy, film posters were traditionally painted—usually a dramatization of events in the film and larger-than-life images of the stars—by such masters as the prolific Anselmo Ballester, Ercole Brini, Luigi Martinati and Alfredo Capitani. This tradition carried over to the posters of the New Wave, which were frequently mainstream (if dramatically heightened) treatments of the film's plot and stars. Averardo Ciriello's poster for *Alphaville* is one of the more interesting examples of the genre. He uses a portrait of Anna Karina to sub-divide the poster between a more traditional scene illustration and a black and white pen-sketch of Eddie Constantine. In a medium and country obsessed with the advertising punch of bold colour, Ciriello's inclusion of the black and white portrait was a unusual and rare choice but one that has a deliberate, striking effect.

Ciriello was known for his comic and poster art. He started out in magazine illustration, doing pin-ups for Italian erotic comics. After the Second World War, he focussed on film poster design and his work from this period includes some of the best examples of the artform. He is particularly remembered for his posters for *Spellbound* (1945), *From Russia with Love* (1963) and *Thunderball* (1965).

UN FILM DI

JEAN-LUC GODARD

AGENTE **LEMMY CAUTION:**
MISSIONE ALPHAVILLE

EDDIE CONSTANTINE - ANNA KARINA

AKIM TAMIROFF   HOWARD VERNON

UNA COPRODUZIONE FILM STUDIO S.p.A., Roma - CHAUMIANE PRODUCTION, Paris

Alphaville (1965), Italian two sheet

bedřich dlouhý

(b.1932 Pilsen, Czechoslovakia)

The Polish poster school strongly influenced poster design in other countries of the Eastern Bloc, including Czechoslovakia. Inspired by their Polish counterparts, Czech film poster artists like Zdenêk Ziegler, Milan Grygor, Josef Vylet'al and Bedřich Dlouhý developed their own unique visual language. It referenced their country's own culture and history while playing with a new, experimental meshing of different art forms, typography and bold graphics.

Bedřich Dlouhý's design for *Hiroshima, mon amour* integrates detailed graphics with photography. The poster won an honorable mention at the Czech International Film Posters

Exhibition in 1964 and reflects Dlouhý's inventiveness and mastery of his art. His work is richly expressive, exploring multiple themes through a variety of artistic media.

A painter, graphic artist, typographer, ceramicist and teacher, Dlouhý studied at the Vocational School of Ceramics and the Academy of Fine Arts in Prague. He was a founding member of the influential Šmidrové Group, set up in 1954, which explored the ideas of Dadaism and the aesthetics of strangeness. In the 1960s, his artistic focus was on film posters, creating some of the most admired works in the field during this time. In addition

to *Hiroshima, mon amour*, his most celebrated posters include *Rashomon* (1950, but for 1970's release), *8½* (1963) and *Red Desert* (1964). In 1965, he won the main prize for painting at the International Biennale of Youth in Paris, and in 1996 he received a gold medal from Prague Academy of Fine Art for his work in reforming the school after the fall of the communist regime. Solo exhibitions of his work have been mounted and his paintings and posters are held in institutions and private collections around the world.

HIROŠIMA, MÁ LÁSKA

FRANCOUZSKÝ
FILM
REŽISÉRA
ALAINA
RESNAISE

Hiroshima, mon amour (1960), Czechoslovakian one sheet

benny stilling

(dates and information unknown)

Les Quatre cents coups (1959), Danish pressbook cover

boris grinsson

(1907 Pskov, Russia—1999 Veneux-les-Sablons, France)

A master of realistic illustration in the older, pre-war style, Boris Grinsson created the poster for the French release of *Les Quatre cents coups*. For Truffaut's semi-autobiographical account of a troubled youth who runs away from his family, the artist depicted the tousle-haired boy forlorn on a windswept beach where his escape finally leads him. Grinsson's poster is a direct illustration of the final frame of the film, evoking both sympathy and ambivalence: where is he to go next?

Grinsson was born in Russia. Fleeing the Bolshevik Revolution, his family relocated to Estonia and Grinsson studied art in the Estonian city of Tartu. Moving to Berlin in 1929, he initially harboured acting ambitions before redirecting his energies into designing film posters for the UFA film studio. In 1933, Grinsson was forced to flee Germany after drawing an anti-Nazi election poster that depicted a caricature of Hitler as the Angel of Death. Settling in France, Grinsson continued to pursue film poster design. Post-war, he became one of the major names working in Paris, alongside contemporaries René Péron and Roger Soubie. At this time, Grinsson would often design the alternative 'style B' poster, while another artist, like Péron or Soubie, would design the main poster for a film's release. In 1947, Grinsson helped establish a union of film poster designers. He was one of the most sought-after talents in the business. From the 1930s to 1972 (when he retired from the increasingly photographic profession), Grinsson produced some 1800 posters across a variety of genres. His many notable works include *This Gun For Hire* (1942), *Gilda* (1946), *The Lady from Shanghai* (1948) and *From Russia with Love* (1963).

Les Quatre cents coups (1959), French one sheet

bruno rehak

(1910 Prague, Poland—1977 Frankfurt am Main, Germany)

Zazie dans le métro (1960), German one sheet

Vivre sa vie (1962), German one sheet

carlantonio longi

(1921 Livorno, Italy—1980 Sinalunga, Italy)

Italian film poster artists were renowned for their use of realistic portraiture and detailed key scenes in bright colours. Carlantonio Longi broke with the establishment with his designs for *Hiroshima, mon amour* and *Les Amants*. His bold decision on both artworks to use an intense close-up created an almost abstract graphic and his unusual use of black and white intensified the posters' impact. For *Hiroshima*, he turns the curve of Eiji Okada's back into the mushroom cloud of the nuclear explosion to powerful effect. In his poster for *Les Amants*, the clasping hands of Jeanne Moreau and Jean-Marc Bory manage to convey both the lovers' intense passion, and also the decisive strength that leads Jeanne Moreau's character to walk out on her mediocre marriage for a fresh start with her new lover.

Carlantonio Longi was an important talent in Italian film poster design between the 1940s and 1970s. Some of his most well-known posters include *The Wizard of Oz* (1939, for 1948 release), and Antonioni's *L'Avventura* (1960). He studied at the Art Institute of Florence and the Academy of Fine Arts in Rome, then started working for film distribution companies. Longi's posters for *Hiroshima, mon amour* and *Les Amants* demonstrate his ability to use a minimum of elements to maximum effect and in the late 1960s, he shifted his career into advertising and graphic design. In the 1970s, Longi devoted himself almost exclusively to painting.

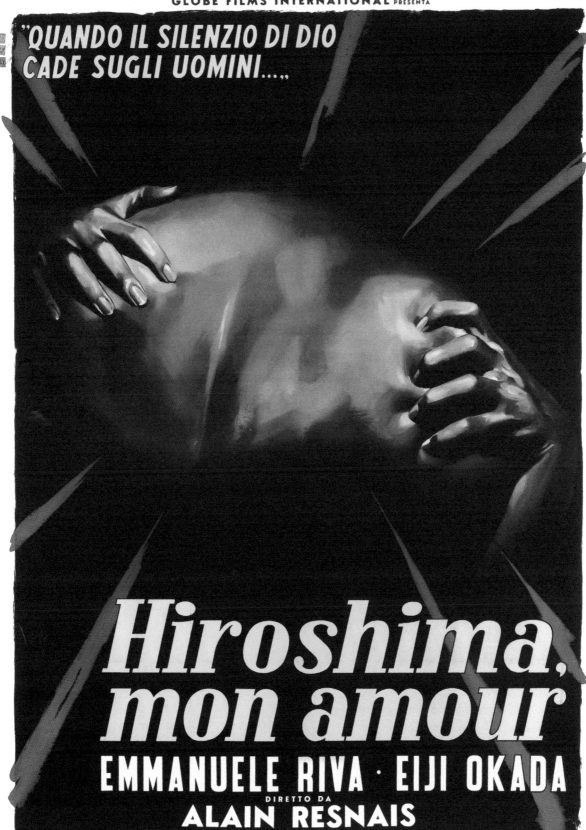

Hiroshima, mon amour (1960), Italian four sheet

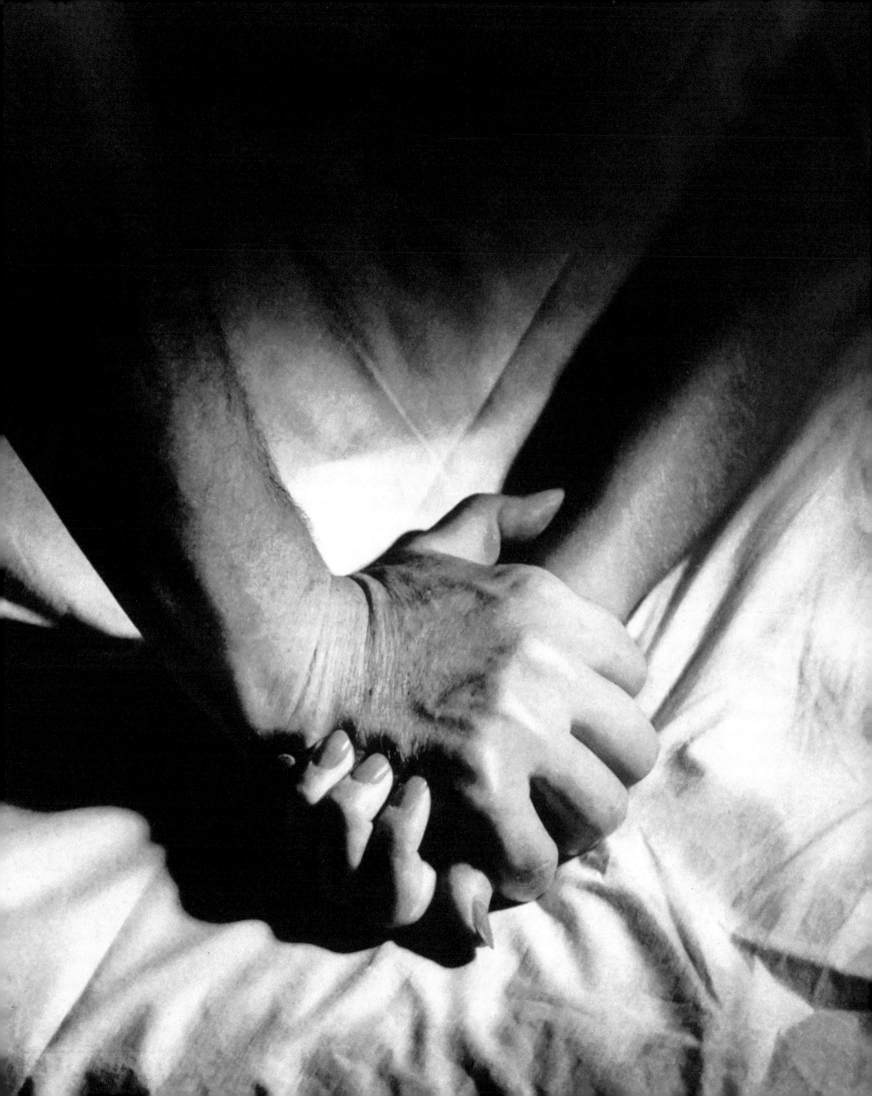

Les Amants (1958), Italian four sheet

chica

(b.1933, France)

Poster artist Chica (Marcel Chikhanovitch) worked with the film's director Jacques Demy on the poster for *Les Parapluies de Cherbourg*. Demy was very particular about the choice of photograph used and the artist then superimposed this onto a bright blue background. He turns the background lettering into notes on a stave, reflecting the musical aspect of the film. Chica worked on a number of other New Wave posters, often in collaboration with the director, including *Une Femme est une femme*, *Cléo de 5 à 7* and *Une Femme douce*.

Chica studied at the National School of Arts and Crafts in Paris, graduating in 1955. In the 1960s, he mainly worked on film posters and then in the late 1960s moved into writing and illustrating children's books and creating tapestries. A number of solo exhibitions of his work have been held.

Les Parapluies de Cherbourg (1962), French one sheet

christian broutin

(b.1933 Chartres, France)

Christian Broutin had an illustrious career as an artist of film posters, advertisements and book illustration. After graduating from the National School of Applied Arts and Crafts in 1951, he began working under the poster artist René Ferracci (see p.238) and designed his first film poster at the age of 21 for Fair Wind to Java (1954). He created over 100 film posters over the next 12 years. He has won several awards for his commercial work and paintings, including the 1983 prize for best French poster design. Two of Broutin's most celebrated works were for the New Wave Pickpocket and Jules et Jim.

Broutin's design for Pickpocket was not used for the main promotional campaign and was only shown on a small French poster. Of all his film posters, it was apparently Broutin's personal favourite and can be viewed from today's vantage point as embodying the best of twentieth century graphic design.

Broutin's poster for Jules et Jim won him the Toulouse-Lautrec poster prize in 1962. The film centres on the unpredictable, enigmatic Catherine (Jeanne Moreau) who keeps vacillating between two close friends— the German Jules (Oskar Werner) and the Frenchman Jim (Henri Serre). The image of Moreau dominates Broutin's poster. Truffaut struggles to make the character of Catherine sympathetic, with her sudden irrational outbursts and impulsive destructive energies. Broutin's portrait reveals the complexity of her personality; he foregrounds her beauty but also implies a darker nature. Combining an illustrated coat with a photographic face, he creates an aura of mysterious sensuality with luminous red hair swirling around her like a surreal halo. The exuberance of her smile is contrasted by the feverishly crisscrossed black strokes on her jacket, while the fine lines on her clasped hands reveal her fragility and vulnerability.

Pickpocket (1959), French mini sheet

Jules et Jim (1962), French one sheet

clément hurel

(1927 Nancy, France—2008 Paris, France)

Clément Hurel was one of the most prolific poster artists in France, responsible for over 1500 posters throughout his career. He was also a passionate advocate of the rights of poster designers, dedicated to fighting the abuse of intellectual copyright and the uncredited use of artists' work.

For À bout de souffle, Hurel created two strikingly different posters. Godard's pastiche of the American gangster genre follows a petty criminal (Jean-Paul Belmondo) who casually shoots a policeman, is betrayed by his American girlfriend, and is finally killed in the street when he attempts to escape the police. One poster is a combination of brushwork and integrated typography; the other is photographic. The former illustrates the final scene of the film in which the police shoot Belmondo in the back. The sketched, monochrome-blue rendering of Belmondo's figure is contrasted with a colorful close-up of Seberg's face that dominates the upper section of the poster. While his lips seem to be searching hers, her gaze is averted elusively. One critic actually suggested that, 'Michel . . . living as he imagines Bogart would, dies because his girlfriend wants to play Bogart as well.' The striking typography of the title is part of the composition: the first letter of each word is boxed in a square or rectangle which, together with the framed image of Seberg, form an abstract grid from which the main character cannot escape.

The alternate style poster for the film is one of Hurel's most recognised works and features a black and white cropped photograph of Belmondo and Seberg kissing. It is one of the best examples of the use of photomontage in poster design—a technique favoured by the poster artists of the New Wave. Hurel uses a seemingly simple stylistic devise—rotating the photo of Belmondo and Seberg kissing and the film's title counterclockwise—to great effect. This twist is jarring and intended: is the couple fighting or loving each other?

Adieu Philippine (1962), French tearsheet

UN FILM DE JEAN-LUC GODARD

HUREL.

LE PETIT
SOLDAT

PRODUCTION GEORGES DE BEAUREGARD · S.N.C.
4, rue de CERISOLES · PARIS-8e · ELY 99.84 · BAL. 06.55

LA SOCIÉTÉ NOUVELLE
DE CINÉMATOGRAPHIE
présente

ANNA KARINA
MICHEL SUBOR
dans un film de
JEAN-LUC GODARD

LE PETIT SOLDAT

Une co-production
GEORGES DE BEAUREGARD
SOCIÉTÉ NOUVELLE DE CINÉMA

HUREL.

un film de Jean-Luc Godard
avec
Anna Karina
Michel Subor
image de Raoul Coutard
production G. de Beauregard. S. N. C.
4 rue de Cerisoles. Paris - ELY. 99-84

(All) *Le Petit Soldat* **(1963), French tearsheet**

constantin films

Das neue Werk des französischen Meisterregisseurs ALAIN RESNAIS des Schöpfers von „Hiroshima mon amour"

Letztes Jahr in Marienbad

Mit diesem Film beginnt eine neue Epoche der Filmkunst! Ausgezeichnet mit dem höchsten Preis der Internationalen Filmfestspiele Venedig 1961

Es spielen: Giorgio Albertazzi · Delphine Seyrig · Sacha Pitoëff

Drehbuch und Dialoge: Alain Robbe-Grillet Eine französisch-italienische Co-Produktion im Verleih *Constantin-Film*

L'Année dernière à Marienbad (1961), German one sheet, side A

The German distribution, and later production, company Constantin Filmverleih GmbH was founded in 1950 by Preben Philipsen and Waldfried Barthel. In the 1950s, Constantin became the distributor for studios including Columbia Pictures and Universal Artists. As well as the more classic mainstream offerings, Constantin also distributed a number of arthouse films. Moving into the 1960s, this included a number of French New Wave releases. Constantin took an unusual approach to marketing these films, printing high-quality double-sided posters and employing different artists to create the design for each side, often balancing a more classic take on one side with a contemporary approach on the reverse. This left cinema managers free to choose how best to represent the film to their local audience. There were very few of these posters printed and they were only produced for a short period of time before Constantin reverted to the more traditional (and budget-friendly) single-sided poster.

L'Année dernière à Marienbad (1961), German one sheet, side B

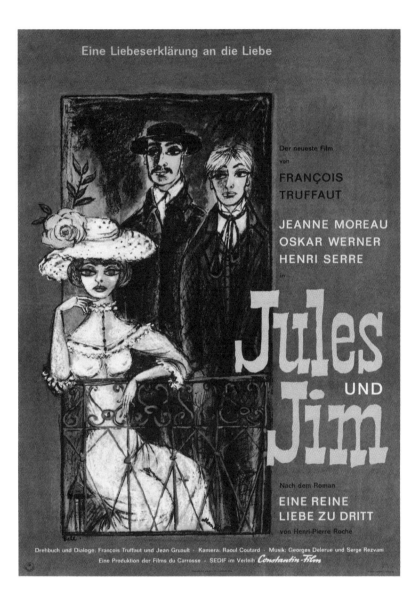

Jules et Jim (1962), German one sheet, side A

Jules et Jim (1962), German one sheet, side B

PIERRE BRAUNBERGER presenta **ANNA KARINA** SADY REBBOT

QUESTA È LA MIA VITA
un film di JEAN-LUC GODARD

PREMIO SPECIALE DELLA GIURIA E PREMIO
DELLA CRITICA AL XXIII° FESTIVAL DI VENEZIA

Vivre sa vie (1962), Italian four sheet

enrico de seta

(1908 Catania, Italy—2008 Rome, Italy)

Italian cinematographic painter Enrico De Seta had a gift for portraiture and capturing the nuance of a single scene. His artwork for Truffaut's *Quatre cents coups* brought these talents to the fore, augmented by an astute use of colour, highlighting the boy's remoteness from his parents and the adults he encounters.

De Seta was working as a draftsman from the age of 15, and a few years later co-founded a student satirical magazine, *Il Cerino*, going on to work for various newspapers and magazines as a satirical cartoonist. He was friends with the director Federico Fellini and in 1945 they set up the 'Funny Face' shop in Rome, painting caricatures for soldiers when they arrived in the city. De Seta had designed his first film poster for *La Grande Illusion* in 1937 but it was not until the 1950s that this became his main focus.

Over the course of his prolific career, he worked on over 1000 poster campaigns, including the Fellini classics *I Vitelloni* (1953) and *La Strada* (1954). In 1953, he won the Spiga Cambellotti prize for best cinematographic painter of the year and in 1995 he was awarded the Order of Merit Commander of the Italian Republic. He lived until he was 100.

Les Quatre cents coups (1959), Italian two sheet

ercole brini

(1913 Rome, Italy—1989 Rome, Italy)

Ercole Brini studied at Rome's Academy of Fine Arts. From the early 1940s he focussed on cinematographic art and developed a reputation as one of the best in his field. He worked on campaigns for films including *Bicycle Thieves* (1948), *To Catch a Thief* (1955) and *Breakfast at Tiffany's* (1961).

Brini was renowned for his distinctive watercolour style that often revealed the delicate emotions that lay behind the surface of characters' faces, as seen in his depiction of Delphine Seyrig and Giorgio Albertazzi in *L'Année dernière à Marienbad*. Brini was an Italian poster artist and this is one of the only French posters he worked on.

L'Année dernière à Marienbad (1961), French one sheet

everett aison

(b.1934 Amsterdam, New York, USA)

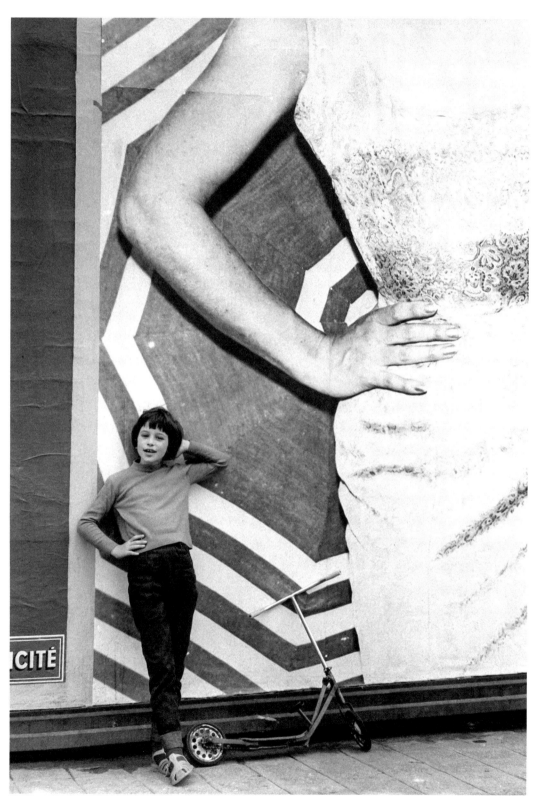

When (and if) the films of the French New Wave were given an American release, they were typically shown in a handful of arthouse cinemas and distributed by small independent companies. Louis Malle's *Zazie dans le Métro* was distributed by the fledgling Seneca International. One of the company's partners, William Kronick, asked his good friend Everett Aison to design the film's poster. He uses the lettering of the film's title to simple and striking effect as the Eiffel Tower. American film posters were at this time very traditional and Aison's stripped back, graphic approach was resoundingly modern. The use of only three colours—those of the French flag—had the added benefit of being low-budget and cheaper to print. Aison brought his minimal designs to posters for Seneca's American versions of a number of foreign imports, such as Kurosawa's *Yojimbo* (1961) and Polanski's *Knife in the Water* (1962). He also created and designed the opening titles for these films (Aison had first started designing titles for his friends' short films at the School of Visual Arts, including Kronick's *A Bowl of Cherries*.)

Aison studied illustration at Syracuse University and worked for the college newspaper as a cartoonist. He served in Korea from 1956 to 1958 then attended the School of Visual Arts in New York in 1959 in the typography department. He was mentored by the school's co-founder, Silas H. Rhodes, who invited him to teach graphic design. Aison started a film school within the School of Visual Arts, which he ran for nearly 40 years, establishing its worldwide reputation for excellence. He was also the art director at Grossman Publishers; has authored a number of successful screenplays; written a novel, *Artrage*; and illustrated two children's books, one of which, *Arthur*, was originally released in 1962, but given a fresh re-release in 2015.

LOUIS MALLE'S **ZAZIE**

"AN EXCEEDINGLY
FUNNY PICTURE.
A REMARKABLE
FRENCH FILM."
GILL, THE NEW YORKER

A SENECA INTERNATIONAL LTD. RELEASE IN EASTMANCOLOR

Zazie dans le Métro (1960), American one sheet

franciszek starowieyski

(1930 Bratkówka, Poland—2009 Warsaw, Poland)

Franciszek Starowieyski created some of the most powerful and expressive posters of the French New Wave. The artist once commented that 'The viewer expects the artist to scandalize, insult and shock him.' Rendered in a dense palette, his posters are rich in metaphor, black humour and the grotesque; at the heart of his practice lay a deep fascination with death and the human body, with artists like Peter Paul Rubens deliberate inspirations.

One of the most distinctive and esteemed artists of the Polish poster school, Starowieyski studied painting at the Krakow Academy of Fine Arts and then at the Warsaw Academy of Fine Arts, graduating in 1955 just as the film poster was emerging as a serious art form in the country. He designed some 300 posters and had numerous exhibitions of his work, including being the first Pole to have a solo exhibition at the Museum of Modern Art (MoMA) in New York in 1985. His posters won several awards, including the film poster award at the Cannes Film Festival in 1974, the Gold Plaque at the International Film Festival in Chicago in 1979 and the International Biennale of Posters in Warsaw in 1978 and 2000. He was also a respected theatre set designer and created the impressive Theatre of Drawing productions, which saw large-format compositions created in front of an audience.

La Mariée était en noir (1968), Polish one sheet

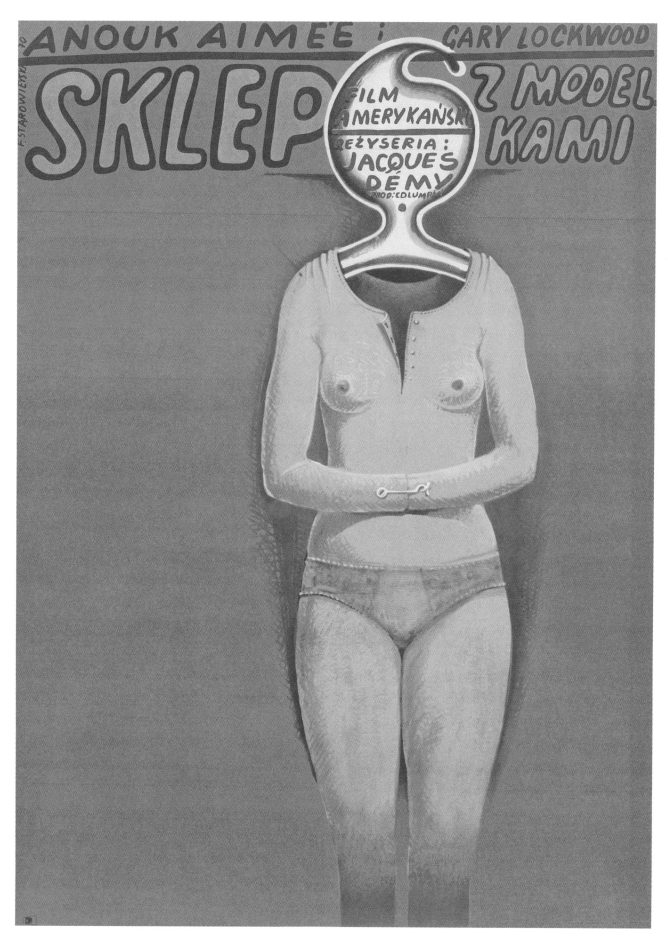

Model Shop (1969), Polish one sheet

Une Femme est une femme (1961), Polish one sheet

georges allard

(dates unknown)

Godard's biggest box office success and the most accessible of his films, *Le Mépris* was a tale of filmmaking and marital breakdown set in the glorious surroundings of Capri in Italy. George Allard's rich use of colour for the French poster reflects the lavish, sun-soaked Technicolor of the film. Taking a more traditional, painterly approach to film poster design than many of the artists associated with the New Wave, he also foregrounds the obvious sensuality of its star, Brigitte Bardot. Professionally active from the 1940s to 1960s, Gilbert 'Georges' Allard produced over 80 film posters, most of them for Jacques Fourastié's advertising agency, including *Red River* (1948), *Baby Doll* (1956) and *Black Orpheus* (1959).

le sexe
et la
jeunesse
de la
France
d'aujourd'hui

d'après G. KERFYSER

Columbia
INTERDIT AUX MOINS DE 18 ANS

Visa Ministériel n° 2063

Masculin Féminin

de
JEAN-LUC GODARD
avec
CHANTAL GOYA et JEAN-PIERRE LEAUD

UNE COPRODUCTION FRANCO-SUEDOISE
ANOUCHKA FILMS - ARGOS FILMS - PARIS
SVENSK FILMINDUSTRI - SANDREWS - STOCKHOLM

ATELIERS LALANDE - WISSOUS (S.-et-O.) 628.98 C.

Masculin Féminin (1966), French half sheet

MACHA
MERIL

dans un film de
JEAN-LUC
GODARD

une femme
mariée

avec
PHILIPPE LEROY
Le mari

et BERNARD NOEL
L'amant

Une co-production ANOUCHKA FILMS · ORSAY FILMS   distribuée par COLUMBIA   INTERDIT aux MOINS de 18 ANS

Une Femme mariée (1964), French one sheet

Deux hommes dans Manhattan (1959), French half sheet

Le Mépris (1963) , Italian four sheet

grove press

Grove Press was one of the most experimental and groundbreaking publishers of the twentieth century, run by the legendary Barney Rosset. Established in New York's Greenwich Village in 1949 by John Balcomb and Robert Phelps, it was purchased two years later by Rosset. By the early 1960s, he had grown Grove's list to include over 500 titles, introducing American audiences to works by writers like William S. Burroughs, Henry Miller, Jean Genet, Tom Stoppard and Harold Pinter in affordable paperbacks; pushing boundaries on accepted notions of decency, morality and sex with erotic literature and previously banned books like *Lady Chatterley's Lover*; and using its publications to drive discussions on politics, civil rights and the counterculture.

In 1967 Grove set up their Film Division,

buying Cinema 16, the 20-year-old New York film society founded by Amos and Marcia Vogel. Cinema 16 gave Grove access to an archive of experimental films, documentaries and classics from both America and beyond and also allowed them to obtain feature films from around the world in line with their vision and outlook. By 1970, the Film Division included over 400 titles. Grove employed Amos Vogel as film editor on their *Evergreen* magazine and as a film consultant. When he was hired, Vogel said of Grove that he believed they had 'the potential to become a major force for modern cinema in America. This movement— encompassing Godard as well as Brakhage, the avant-garde and the independents, the young political filmmakers as well as the explorers of a new aesthetic—requires new patterns of

distribution, exhibition, production and publicity, a willingness to utilise new technological tools and an openness to the "sub-version" of established, already ossified norms and techniques.' He was instrumental in establishing the Grove Press International Film Festival in 1970. Vogel organised 12 Grove features to be screened at three New York venues in March, including Alain Robbe-Grillet's French-Czechoslovakian drama *L'Homme qui ment* and William Klein's French satire *Mr. Freedom*. Grove also used the festival to simultaneously release all 12 films at arthouse cinemas and universities across the country. The posters for the Festival films were created by in-house artists at Grove Press and were uncredited.

L'Homme qui ment (1968), American special sheet for Grove Press International Film Festival (1970)

A Grove Press International Film Festival Presentation
Starring Donald Pleasance, Delphine Seyrig and John Abbey ■ Film by William Klein – An O.P.E.R.A., Paris Film

Mr. Freedom (1969), American one sheet for Grove Press International Film Festival (1970)

györgy kemény

(b.1936 Budapest, Hungary)

The influential György Kemény was an innovative figure in Hungarian graphic art from the 1960s to 1980s. He was particularly celebrated for being one of the first artists to introduce Pop Art to Hungary and for his skill in typography, strengths evident in his design for Truffaut's *Fahrenheit 451*, based on Ray Bradbury's classic dystopian novel.

Kemény had studied poster design working in Pál Gábor's studio for a year (this was after he had initially been rejected by the University of Fine Arts). In 1968, he had a one-man exhibition where he showed a number of his Pop Art paintings. It was very influential and also seen as something of an outrage. Likewise, a number of his commercial posters for swimwear and umbrellas caused a scandal for being too erotic and progressive. It was this ability to push boundaries and bring a fresh, modern approach to graphic design that led to him being classed as one of the most important artists of this period. In the late 1960s, he designed the poster for the renowned Iparterv group exhibition, a significant event in the history of art in Hungary. In 1971, he was part of the Papp Group and their activities. In 1975, he shared first prize with Shigeo Fukuda at the Warsaw Poster Biennale for the 30th anniversary of the Holocaust. In 1986, he took part in and designed the poster for a serious exhibition on the history of Hungarian poster art. Since 2004, he has been a member of the Hungarian Poster Association.

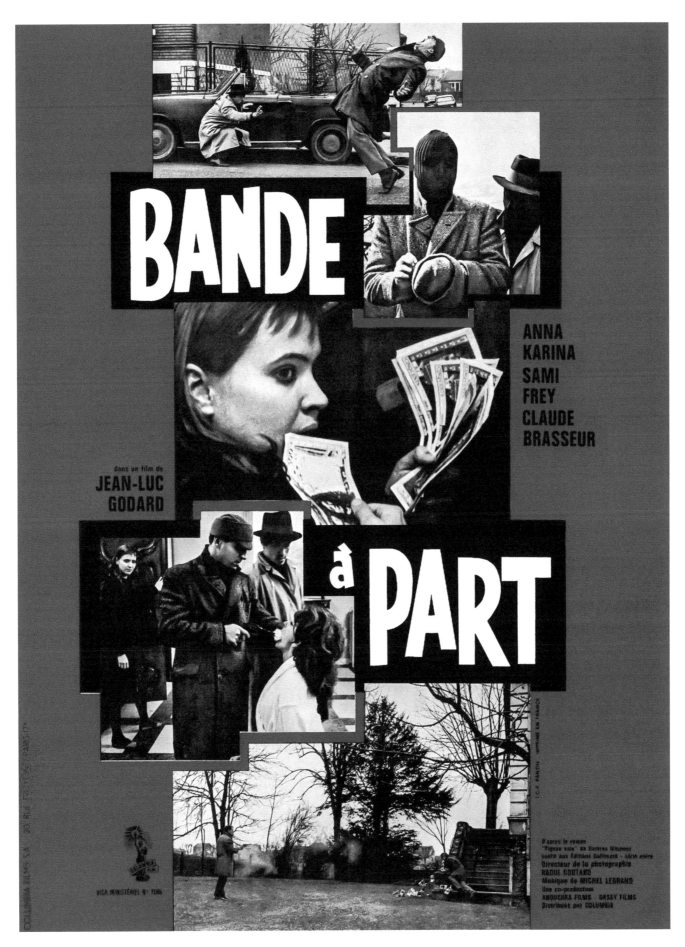

Bande à part (1964), French half sheet

hans hillmann

(1925 Silesia [now Poland]—2014 Frankfurt am Main, Germany)

A master of minimalism, Hans Hillmann was a major force in graphic design in Germany in the 1960s, creating around 130 film posters between the late 1950s and mid 1970s for auteur directors like Antonioni, Cocteau, Fellini, Godard and Kurosawa.

Hillmann studied at the State Art School in Kassel, Germany. As a new graduate, he was approached by the arthouse film distribution company Neu-Filmkunst to design a poster for *Life Begins Tomorrow* (1952). Hillmann's design, featuring a film strip as the profile of a face, proved so popular with the distributor that they used it as their company logo and partnered with the designer on many films over several years. Hillmann also frequently workd with Atlas distribution.

When Hillman secured a new commission, he would watch the film in question repeatedly, taking photographs of various scenes and making meticulous notes and sketches before starting work on his design. He was able to break through surface distractions to interpret the very essence of a film in his key art. A genius of simplicity, his posters were often also in black or white or just two or three colours. This was often because of budgetary constraints but also served to heighten their striking impact.

Hillmann had a long-running relationship with Jean-Luc Godard and designed eight posters for the director. Godard, in turn, included one of Hillman's posters in *Deux ou trois choses que je sais d'elle*. The poster for *Muriel*, featuring a torn notebook, was commissioned by director

Alain Resnais directly from Hillman for the French poster campaign. Of his poster for Louis Malle's *Le Feu follet*, Hillmann commented, 'One usually puts fresh flowers on the grave of a loved one. Here, I put dead leaves on the photo of the main actor while he was still alive.' Hillmann created his most abstract poster for Godard's *Weekend*. The image is reduced to disintegrating typography, which functions as a metaphor for Godard's biting satire about the collapse of a consumer society.

Hillmann was also a prominent professor of graphic arts at the Academy of Fine Arts in Kassel and a member of Arts Council of German Federal Post.

Scene from *Deux ou trois choses que je sais d'elle* with Hillmann's *Muriel* poster on the wall.

Muriel (1963), French half sheet

Le Feu follet (1963), German one sheet

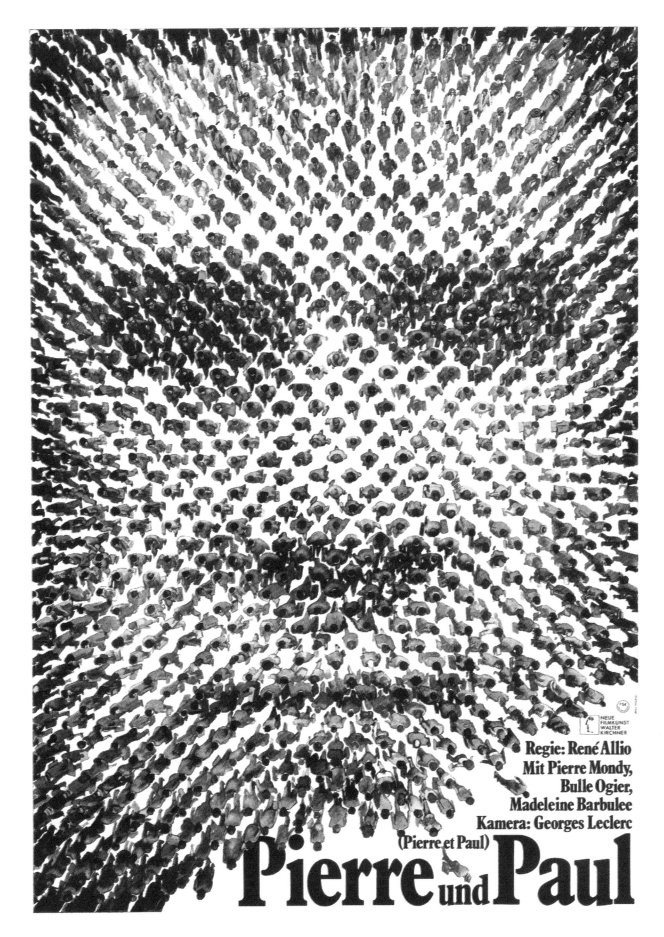

Pierre et Paul (1969), German one sheet

Jean-Luc Godard: Die Geschichte der Nana S.

(Vivre sa vie) Kamera: Raoul Coutard
Darsteller: Anna Karina, Sady Rebbot

Neue
Filmkunst
Walter
Kirchner

Vivre sa vie (1962), German one sheet

Une Femme est une femme (1961), German one sheet

Belle de Jour (1967), German one sheet

Neue Filmkunst
Walter Kirchner zeigt
Den Ideenkrimi der „Neuen
Welle" Buch und Regie:
Jacques Rivette. Mit
Betty Schneider, François
Prévost, Gianni Esposito

PARIS GEHÖRT UNS

(Paris nous appartient)

Paris nous appartient (1961), German one sheet

Mit Mireille Darc,
Jean Yanne,
Daniel Pommereulle,
Jean-Pierre Lèaud,
Jean-Pierre Kalfon

Nach der Mao-roten „Chinoise"
eine hämoglobingetränkte
Geschichte von Rittern der Land-
straße, Normalverbrauchern
und Kannibalen.

Kamera: Raoul Coutard
Prädikat: Besonders wertvoll
Regie und Buch:

Jean-Luc Godard

■ パ リ
脚本・監督 フランソワ・トリュフォー
ジャン・ピエール・レオー
マリー・フランス・ピジエ 主演

■ ロ ー マ
脚本・監督 レンツォ・ロッセリーニ
エレオノラ・ロッシ・ドラゴ
クリスティナ・ガイオーニ 主演

■ 東 京
脚本・監督 石原慎太郎
音楽 武満 徹
田村奈己 古畑弘二
横山道代 主演

■ ミュンヘン
脚本・監督 マルセル・オフュールス
バーバラ・フライ
クリチャン・デルマー
ベラ・チェホワ 主演

■ ワルシャワ
脚本 イェルジー・スタウィンスキー
監督 アンジェイ・ワイダ
バルバラ・ラス
ツビグニエフ・チブルスキー
ウラディスワフ・コワルスキー 主演

×   ×   ×

写真 アンリ・カルティエ・ブレッソン
音楽 ジョルジュ・ドルリュ
歌手 ザビェ・デプラース

シネマスコープ

Neue
Filmkunst
Walter
Kirchner

二十歳の恋

リア・日本・ドイツ・ポーランド ■ピエール・ルースタン作品 東和提供

Week-end (1967), German one sheet

se one sheet

123   hiroyoshi ohshima

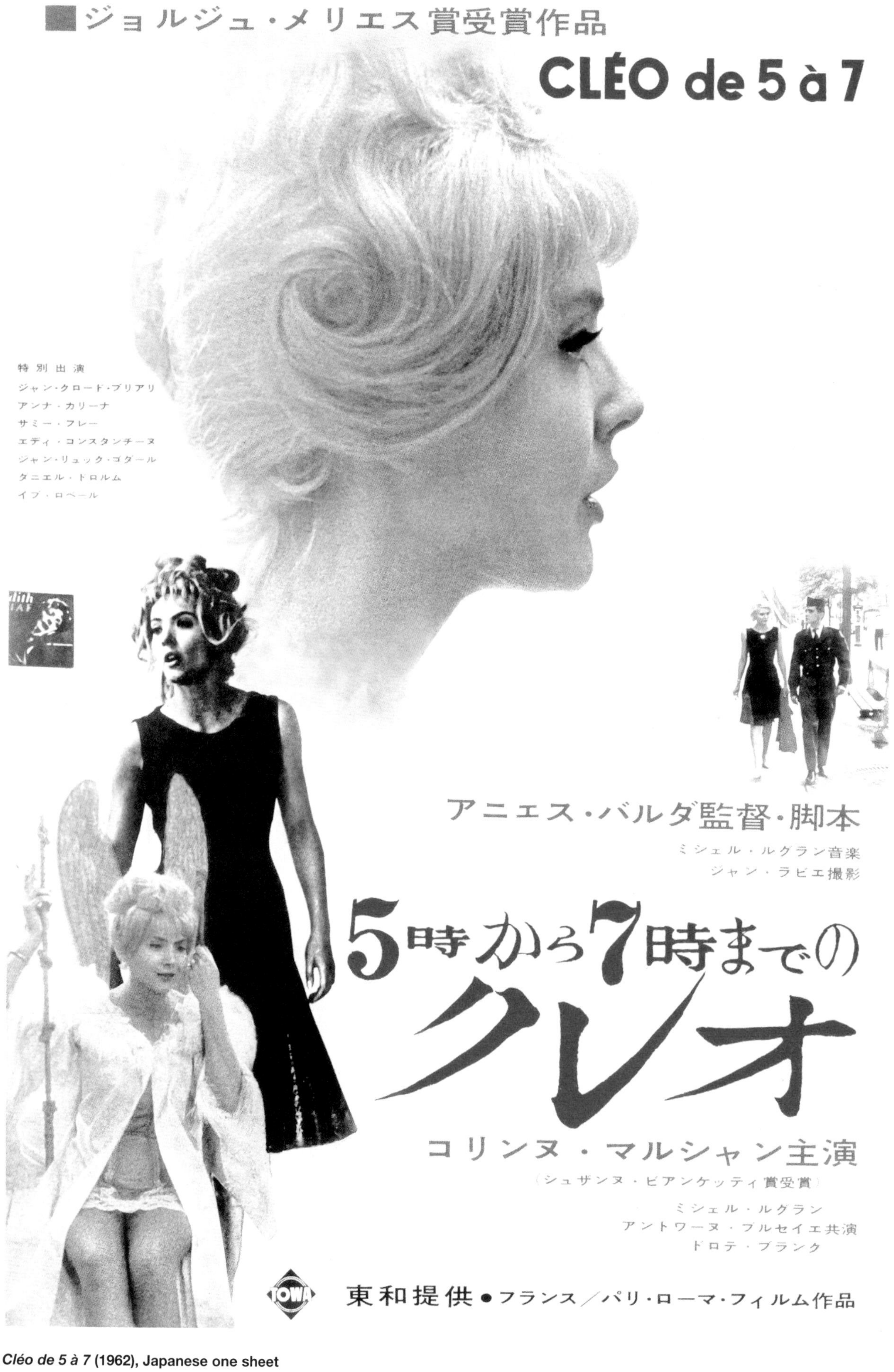

Cléo de 5 à 7 (1962), Japanese one sheet

L'Année dernière à Marienbad (1961), Japanese one sheet

Tirez sur le pianiste (1960), Japanese one sheet

hisamitsu noguchi

(1909 Utsunomiya, Japan—1994)

Les Quatre cents coups (1959), Japanese two sheet

Hisamitsu Noguchi was one of the most distinguished and influential Japanese film poster artists of the twentieth century. He was responsible for two posters for Truffaut's *Quatre cents coups*. His portrait on the one sheet shows an expression on the boy's face that is somehow less vulnerable, more mischievous and defiant than he was depicted in posters from other countries. Noguchi adopts an extremely textured painterly approach in a style almost reminiscent of impressionist art where muted pastel colours and eye-catching Japanese typography combine to create a compelling image. Of all the posters designed for his films, this particular Noguchi artwork was Truffaut's personal favourite and he wrote a letter of appreciation to Noguchi. In reply, Noguchi gifted Truffaut the original artwork.

Noguchi created the posters for over 500 Japanese films over his 50-year career. For many years, he worked at Towa-Toho Film, Japan's oldest and foremost distributor of foreign films. Established in 1928, the company provides Japanese audiences with European and American films ranging from arthouse to blockbuster titles. He created the Japanese posters for critically-acclaimed European films including *Pépé le Moko* (1937), *Children of Paradise* (1945) and *The Third Man* (1949). At the age of 72 he designed a poster for the Bond film *For Your Eyes Only* (1981).

Noguchi was passionate about film with an incredible knowledge base and he was also an avid jazz-enthusiast. He developed a second career as a well-known film and music critic, writing several reviews, articles and books.

Les Quatre cents coups (1959), Japanese one sheet

jacek neugebauer

(b.1934 Sosnowiec, Poland)

Robert Bresson's minimalist tour de force *Au Hasard Balthazar* is profound and moving, frequently cited as one of the greatest films ever made. It is the story of the life of a donkey, Balthazar, from birth to death. Godard commented of it that 'This film is really the world in an hour and a half.' Through the donkey's experiences and the different owners and situations he encounters, Bresson shows the scope of humanity from vile cruelty to purest compassion. The film is deeply spiritual; Bresson never attempts to humanise the donkey and it is through the portrayal of the animal's simple existence that the work becomes transcendent.

The Polish poster for the film was created by Jacek Neugebauer. A graduate of the Warsaw Fine Art Academy, he created over 300 posters between 1963 and 1979 including the well-known designs for *Let's Make Love* (1960) and *Harper* (1966). He won a number of awards and was also renowned for his book illustrations.

Au Hasard Balthazar (1966), Polish one sheet

jacques fourastié

(dates and information unknown)

Le Doulos (1962), French one sheet

Ascenseur pour l'échafaud (1958), French one sheet, style A

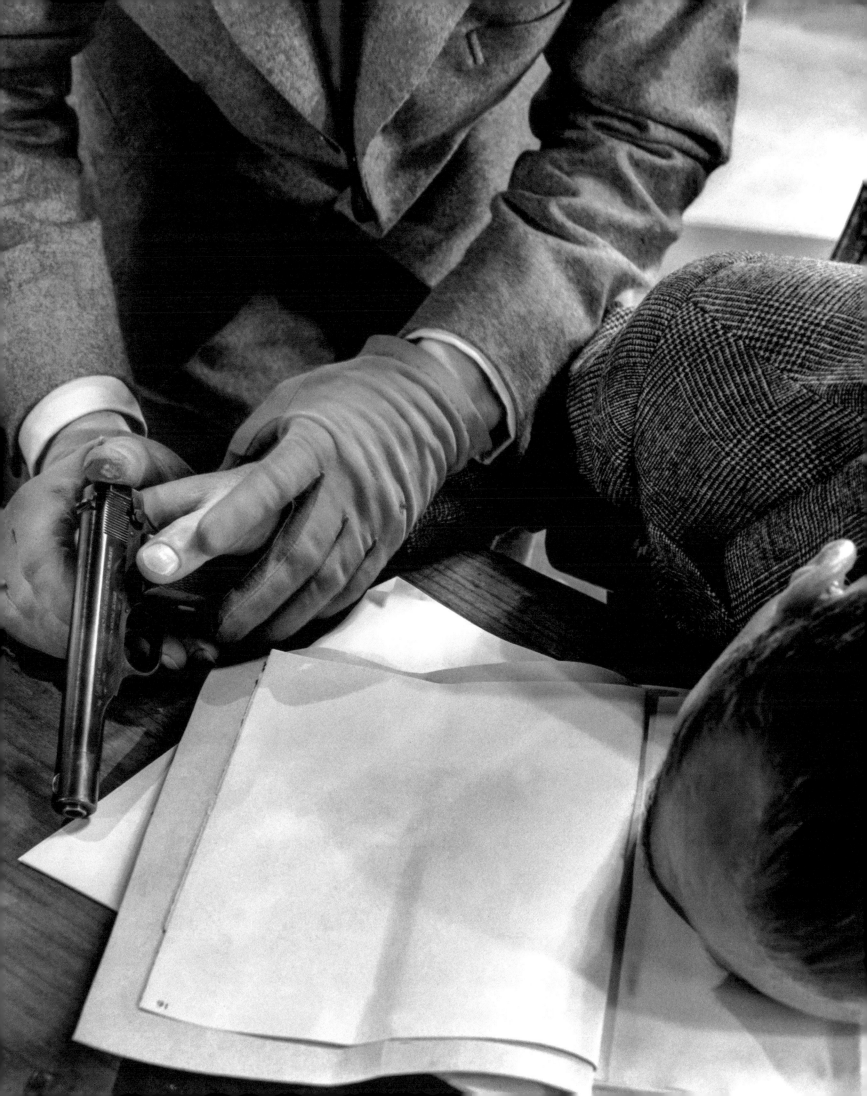

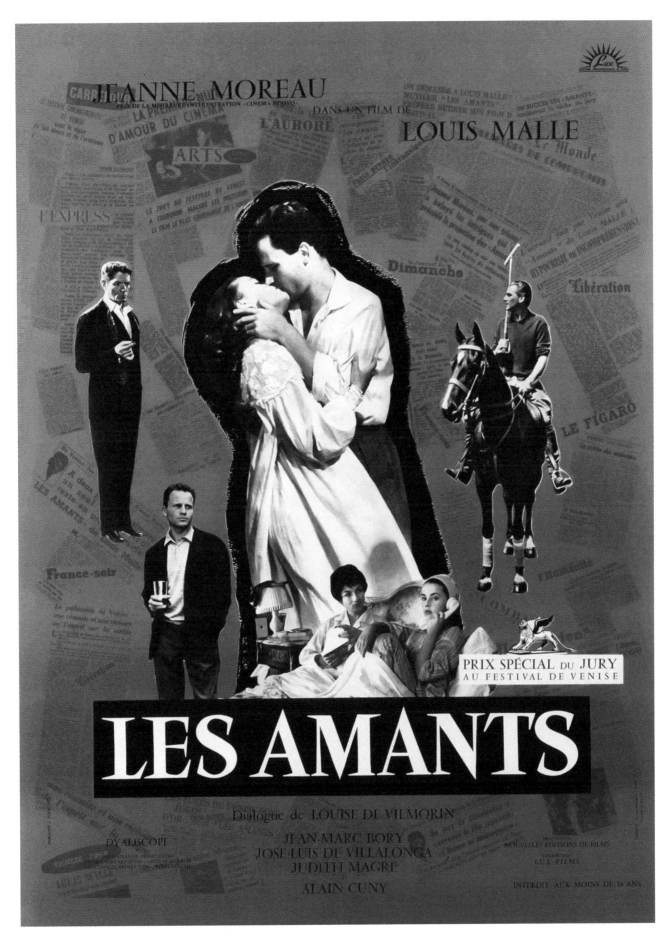

Les Amants (1958), French half sheet

Pickpocket (1959), French one sheet

jacques vaissier

(dates and information unknown)

UN FILM
SUR
LES RELATIONS
ENTRE
BLANCS
ET
NOIRS

LA PYRAMIDE HUMAINE

Un film de
JEAN ROUCH
Production
LES FILMS DE LA PLEIADE

DÉBUT DES PRISES DE VUES LE 25 DÉCEMBRE 1959

La Pyramide humaine (1961), French tearsheet

Vivre sa vie (1962), French tearsheet

Les films de la Pléiade
qui n'en sont pas à
une étoile près
ont choisi Anna
Karina pour jouer
le rôle de Nana
dans Vivre sa vie
un film tourné par
Jean-Luc Godard
et produit, bien
sûr, par Pierre
Braunberger

LES FILMS DE LA PLÉIADE, 95, Champs-Elysees. ELY. 31-64, 32-86 et 51-49

Vivre sa vie (1962), French tearsheet

les films
de la Pléiade
qui n'en sont pas à une
étoile près ont choisi Anna
Karina pour jouer le rôle de
Nana dans Vivre sa vie, un
film tourné par Jean-Luc Godard
et produit, bien sûr, par
Pierre Braunberger.

LES FILMS DE LA PLÉIADE, 95, Champs-Elysées. ELY. 31-64, 32-86 et 51-49

Vivre sa vie (1962), French tearsheet

Le Petit Soldat (1960), French one sheet

Tirez sur le pianiste (1960), French tearsheet

jan lenica

(1928 Poznań, Poland—2001 Berlin, Germany)

Jan Lenica was apparently the first of the groundbreaking group of 1950s Polish artists to coin the phrase 'Polish School of Poster'. He was a respected cartoonist, graphic designer and animated filmmaker. His posters were often characterised by an abstract simplicity that used colour and satirical metaphor in an almost childlike approach. A distorted human figure or head was a recurrent motif.

Lenica originally studied music and architecture before beginning a career in illustration, drawing cartoons for satirical magazines. He began designing movie posters in the early 1950s and won the state award for lithography while he was still in his twenties. He designed over 150 posters which, along with his innovative animated films, have won awards and been exhibited around the world.

Two of the posters Lenica created for the French New Wave show the breadth of his artistry. In his poster for Louis Malle's first feature *Ascenseur pour l'échafaud*, about a murderer who is caught in a malfunctioning elevator while the police indict him for another crime he did not commit, Lenica opts for an abstract, conceptual approach. He superimposes vertically arranged numbers symbolizing the elevator on a black silhouette of head and shoulders, emphasising the physical and psychological entrapment of the protagonist. In addition, the pattern of black dots resembles a close-up of a newspaper photograph—again stressing that the main character is being 'framed' in a literal and symbolic sense.

Lenica's German poster for Godard's *Le Petit Soldat* presents an abstract figure in anguish—'black and blue'—reflecting the suffering of the main character and speaking to the wider themes of torture and the Algerian War that the film deals with.

Ascenseur pour l'échafaud (1958), Polish one sheet

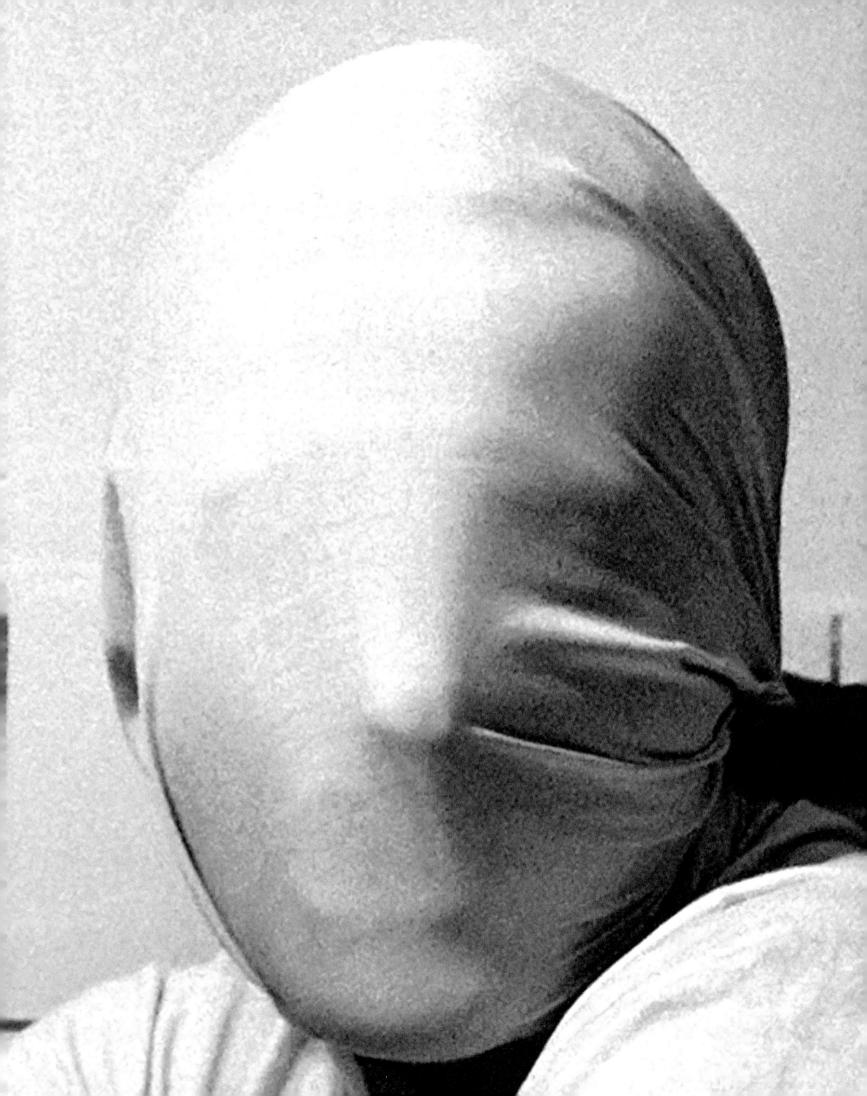

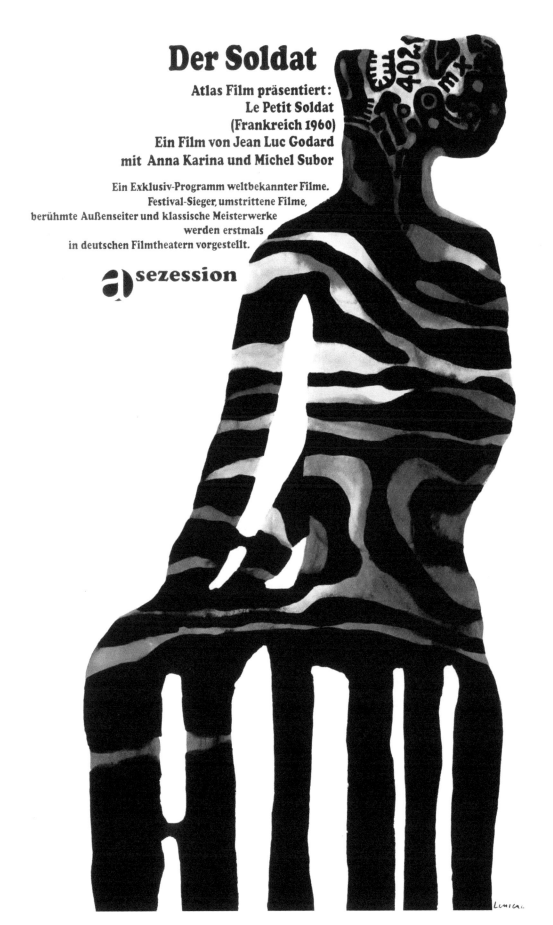

Der Soldat

Atlas Film präsentiert:
Le Petit Soldat
(Frankreich 1960)
Ein Film von Jean Luc Godard
mit Anna Karina und Michel Subor

Ein Exklusiv-Programm weltbekannter Filme.
Festival-Sieger, umstrittene Filme,
berühmte Außenseiter und klassische Meisterwerke
werden erstmals
in deutschen Filmtheatern vorgestellt.

a) sezession

Le Petit Soldat (1963), German one sheet

jan młodożeniec

(1929 Warsaw, Poland—2000 Warsaw, Poland)

The bold use of colour and pleasing simplicity of the Polish poster for *Ma nuit chez Maud* were typical of graphic designer Jan Młodożeniec. Typography was also an important element in his creations, as evidenced by the space given to type in the poster, his own hand-lettering of the title, and the amusing addition of Jean-Louis Trintignant's floating photographic head in his credit.

Młodożeniec was the son of the futurist poet Stanisław Młodożeniec and he studied at the Warsaw Academy of Fine Arts under Henryk Tomaszewski, graduating in 1955. He was an important member of the Polish poster school, responsible for over 400 posters and book covers. He won several awards for his work, including the 1969 award for poster design from the Minister of Culture and Arts; Gold Medal at the International Poster Biennale in 1980; and first prize at the Poster Biennale in 1983. He has held several solo exhibitions and his work is held in private and public collections worldwide, including MoMA in New York, Stedelijk Museum in Amsterdam, and Musée des Arts Décoratifs in Paris.

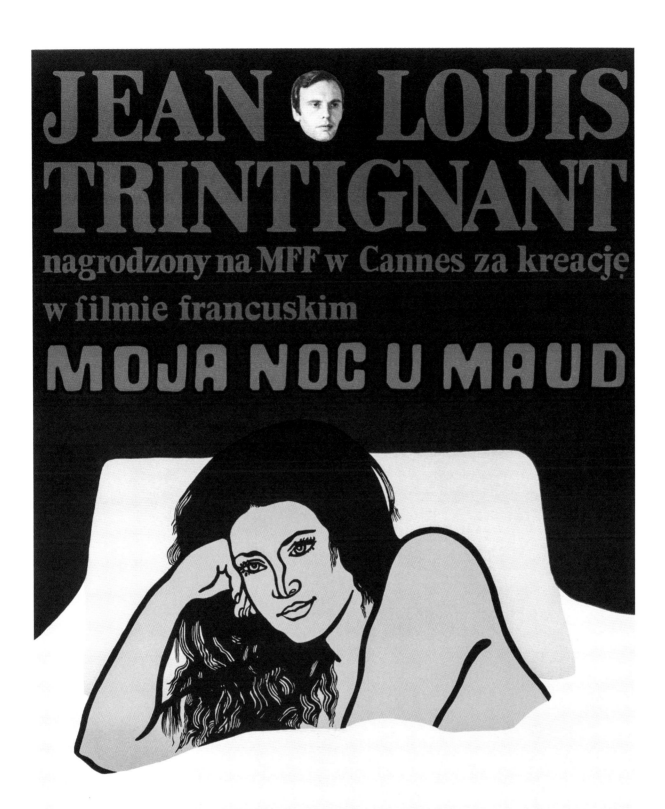

Ma nuit chez Maud (1969), Polish one sheet

janusz rapnicki

(1926 Lublin, Poland—1969)

Little is known of Polish artist Janusz Rapnicki, who died in the late 1960s while still in his early forties. He created a significant body of work for cinema and advertising, including posters for a number of New Wave films like *Les Parapluies de Cherbourg* (1964), *Les Demoiselles de Rochefort* (1967) and *Le Voleur* (1967). As with his poster for *Le Mépris*, he frequently used bright colours, particularly clashing pink and red in his designs—a tip of the hat to Pop Art, Warhol's silkscreens and Blue Note designer Reid Miles. The pink and red was a signature touch of Rapnicki's, combined with a preference for photography and collage.

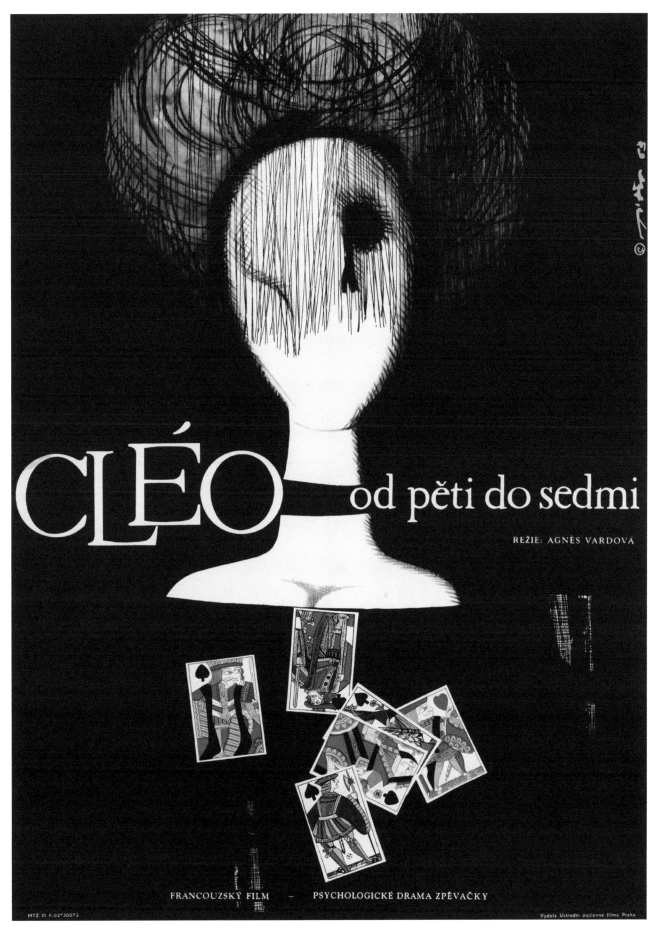

Cléo de 5 à 7 (1962), Czechoslovakian one sheet

jean barnoux

(dates and information unknown)

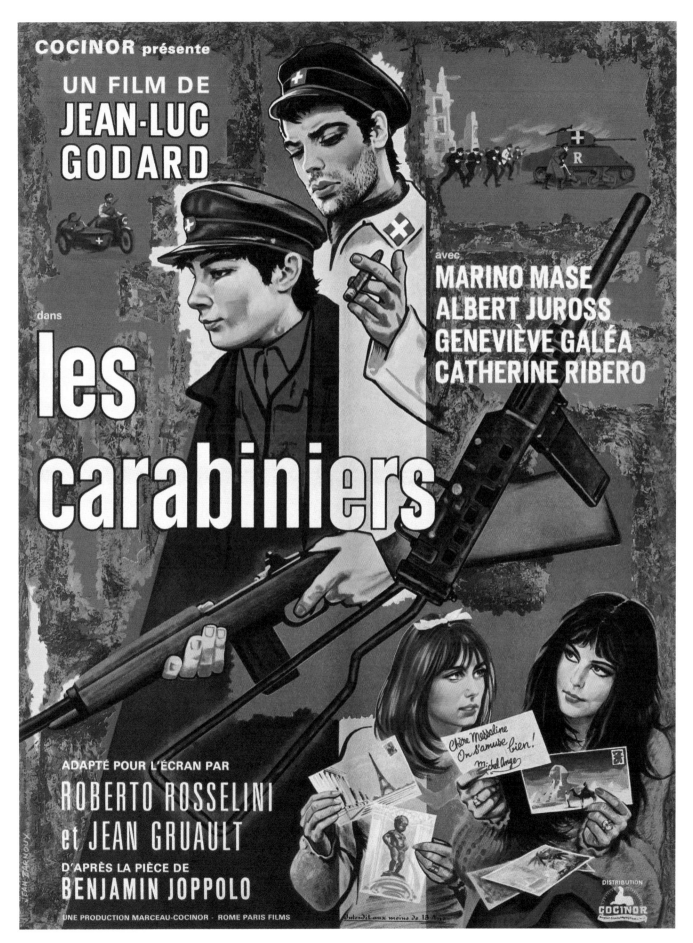

Les Carabiniers (1963), French half sheet

jean cocteau

(1889 Maisons-Laffitte, France—1963 Milly-la-Forêt, France)

Polymath and poet Jean Cocteau was a legendary, larger-than-life figure. A prodigious creator of novels, plays, drawings, sculpture, paintings, poetry and film, he was a major and influential figure in the French avant-garde. Cocteau was passionate about film and his visually mesmerizing creations had a huge influence on the directors of the French New Wave. (Truffaut even produced his *Testament d'Orphée*.)

Le Testament d'Orphée was Cocteau's last film and the final part of his Orphic Trilogy, after *Le sang d'un poète* (1930) and *Orphée* (1950). A poetic, glorious exploration of the relationship between art and its creator, between life and death, the film was made while Cocteau was dying and was a fittingly elegiac, surreal farewell. The cast included several of Cocteau's friends such as Pablo Picasso, Yul Brynner, Jean-Pierre Leáud and Jean Marais.

Naturally, the poster for the film features one of Cocteau's own distinctive paintings. Of his art he once commented that 'poets don't draw, they unravel their handwriting and then tie it up again but differently.'

Le Testament d'Orphée (1960), French mini sheet

jean mascii

(1926 Mirandola, Italy—2003 Paris, France)

As a child in a family of craftsmen, Jean Mascii made detailed miniature theaters. One of his first jobs was in a workshop specialising in cinema facades, where this attention to intricate detail and skill in portraiture led him to eventually focus on film poster design. One of the most prolific artists of his time, Mascii was responsible for more than 2000 film posters and hundreds of book covers over the course of his career, including *Goldfinger* (1964), *The Good, The Bad and the Ugly* (1966) and *Planet of the Apes* (1968). His highly effective poster for *Alphaville* features a portrait of Eddie Constantine and Anna Karina against a detailed dystopian metropolis. The use of black and white serves to further emphasise the noir-esque atmosphere of the film. In a similar vein, his poster for Jean-Pierre Melville's important gangster New-Wave precursor *Bob le flambeur* took an appropriately Noir approach.

Bob le flambeur (1956), French half sheet

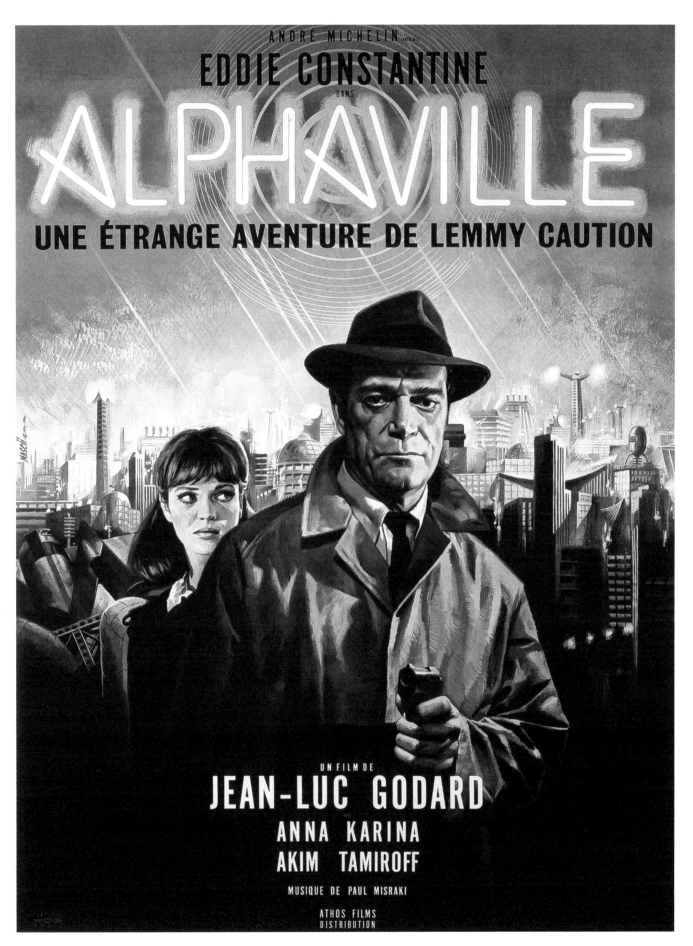

Alphaville (1965), French one sheet

jean-michel folon

(1934 Brussels, Belgium—2005 Monaco)

Jean-Michel Folon was an artist, sculptor and painter. A proponent of the 'less is more' school of design, Folon's deceptively simple approach managed to convey a depth and perception lacking in many of his contemporaries. His use of colour was exquisite and he often favoured shades of blue and purple, as with his poster for *Paris vu par . . .*

Folon studied architecture at the Institut Saint-Luc in Brussels before abandoning the discipline and moving to Paris to paint. He absorbed himself in his art, painting every day for five years and in 1960, he posted some of his illustrations to America. Attracted by his fresh approach yet never having met face to face, *The New Yorker* and *Esquire* published his work. His relationship with both publications would last for several years, alongside other American magazines such as *Time* and *Atlantic Monthly*. In 1966 he was awarded the Certificate of Merit by the Art Directors Club in New York. He held his first solo exhibition at the Lefebre Gallery in New York in 1969 and this led to further exhibitions worldwide, including Tokyo, London and Milan. He illustrated books for Frank Kafka, Ray Bradbury and Jacques Prévert, among others, and designed posters for films and for Amnesty International, Greenpeace and the United Nations. In 1989, he created the birds-in-flight logo used to commemorate the bicentennial of the French Revolution.

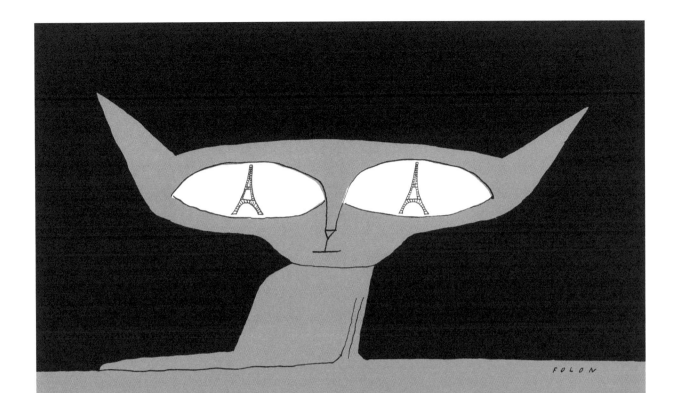

LES FILMS DU LOSANGE BARBET SCHROEDER PRÉSENTENT

PARIS VU PAR

ERIC ROHMER JEAN-LUC GODARD

JEAN DOUCHET CLAUDE CHABROL

JEAN-DANIEL POLLET JEAN ROUCH

EN COULEURS

Paris vu par . . . (1965), French one sheet

jiří hilmar

(b.1937 Hradec Králové, Czechoslovakia)

Jiří Hilmar's design for *À bout de souffle* is unusual in that it only focussed on Jean-Paul Belmondo. Not only is co-star Jean Seberg not pictured, she is also not mentioned in the credits. Despite this, the effect of Hilmar's use of a block colour and simple spiral graphics superimposed onto Belmondo's solitary photographic profile is arresting.

Hilmar studied at the School of Arts and Crafts in Prague in the early 1950s and worked as a successful graphic artist designing film posters—like *Cleopatra* (1963) and *Pierrot le Fou* (1965)—and book jackets throughout the 1950s and 1960s, winning awards for his work. As with *À bout de souffle*, he often used photography combined with a colourwash and geometric elements in his work. In 1967, Hilmar co-founded the Club of Concretists (Klub konkretistů) group of artists. In 1969, he moved to Germany because of the political situation in Czechoslovakia and from 1974 lived in an artists' colony. Major solo exhibitions of his work were held in 1973 in Bochum, Germany and in 1991 in Prague, as well as numerous group shows. From the mid-1970s, Hilmar has increasingly focused on the theme of nature and the threats posed to the natural world by civilisation and the rise of technology.

À bout de souffle (1960), Czechoslovakian one sheet

jiří stach

(b.1944 Prague, Czechoslovakia)

Jiří Stach is a successful Czechoslovakian photographer known for his still lifes and portraits. He has published books on his work, has held several solo exhibitions around the world and his photographs are held in private and public collections. In 2006 he was awarded Personality of Czech Photography by the Association of Czech Photographers. A graduate of the School of Graphic Arts in Prague, Stach also designed several photographic film posters, including the poster for *Alphaville*.

Alphaville (1965), Czechoslovakian one sheet

jolanta karczewska

(b.1933 Warsaw, Poland)

Jolanta Karczewska was one of the few female artists of the Polish Poster School. She had studied under Henryk Tomaszewski at the Academy of Fine Arts in Warsaw and had a successful career in film poster design. She favoured the use of photography, often working in a neutral or black and white palette. In contrast, her poster for Louis Malle's *Zazie dans le Métro* is an illustrated riot of bright colour, reflecting the film's joyful silliness.

Les Quatre cents coups (1959), Czechoslovakian one sheet

jouineau bourduge

Guy Jouineau and Guy Bourduge worked together for over 50 years, creating over 500 film posters. They met studying graphic art in Paris in the late 1940s. After graduation they got their start as professional artists by knocking on the door of the singer Charles Aznavour, who loved their work and introduced them to his record company. They worked on a number of album covers and then designed their first movie poster in 1957 for *Nathalie de Christian-Jaque*. Based from their workshop in Paris, they designed film posters for Pathé then Gaumont and created artwork for films as diverse as *Fellini's Roma* (1972), *La Cage aux Folles* (1978), *One Flew Over the Cuckoo's Nest* (1975) and a number of French New Wave films. Jouineau and Bourduge once commented that Truffaut was not an easy director to work with! They were fluent in many styles, 'We worked in the old-fashioned way, doing photo editing, collage, drawings. It worked well!' In 1990, they won the Cesar award for best film poster for their design for *Cinema Paradiso*.

MIREILLE DARC

JEAN YANNE

DANS UN FILM DE
JEAN-LUC GODARD

Week-end

AVEC
VALERIE LAGRANGE
ET
JEAN-PIERRE KALFON

DIRECTEUR GÉNÉRAL DE LA PRODUCTION RALPH BAUM / DIRECTEUR DE LA PRODUCTION PHILIPPE SENNÉ
DIRECTEUR DE LA PHOTOGRAPHIE RAOUL COUTARD / MUSIQUE ORIGINALE ANTOINE DUHAMEL (ÉDITIONS HORTENSIA)
COPRODUCTION : LES FILMS COPERNIC / COMACICO / LIRA FILMS (PARIS) - ASCOT CINERAD (ROME)
EASTMANCOLOR

PUBL. A. NICARD

Week-end (1967), French one sheet

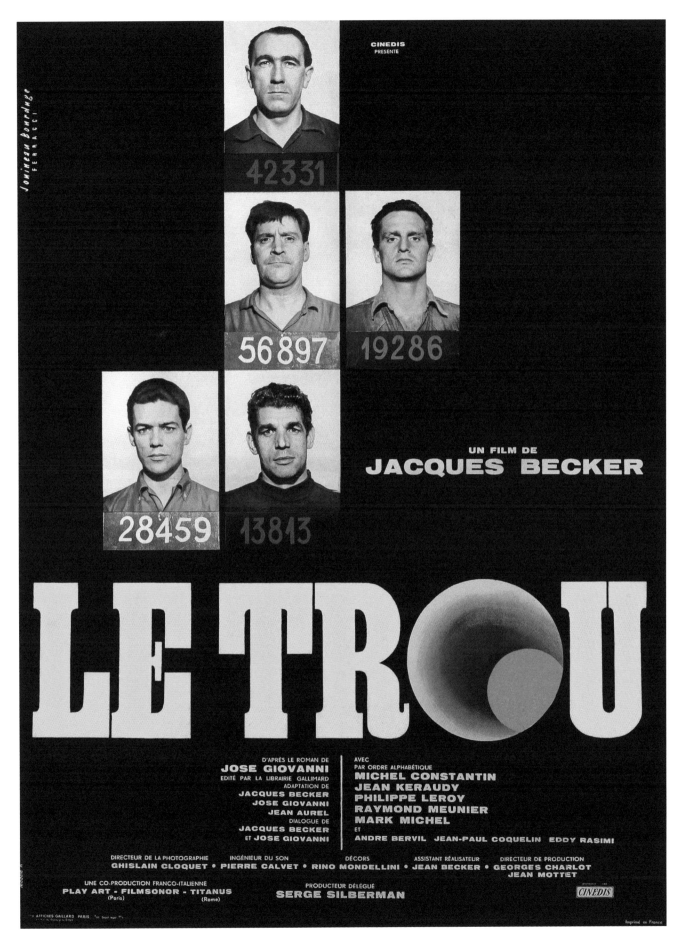

Le Trou (1960), French one sheet, style A

Tirez sur le pianiste (1960), French one sheet

junji aino

(dates and information unknown)

Pierrot le Fou (1965), Japanese one sheet

kazuo kamimura

(1940 Yokosuka City, Japan—1986 Japan)

Les Parapluies de Cherbourg (1964), Japanese horizontal one sheet

Manga artist Kazuo Kamimura was known as Showa No Eshi, which translated means 'Ukiyoe painter of the Showa Era' and was a tribute to his graceful, clean stroke lines. He was also celebrated for his expressive illustrations— especially of women—and was a fitting choice to illustrate the Japanese poster for *Les Parapluies de Cherbourg*.

Kamimura graduated from the Musashino Art University's design department in 1964. He worked at Senkosya advertising agency as an illustrator and also developed his career as a Manga artist. In the early 1970s, Kamimura created the manga *Lady Snowblood* with writer Kazuo Koike, which was serialised in publisher Shueisha's *Weekly Playboy*. *Lady Snowblood* was adapted into a film in 1973 and 30 years later, Quentin Tarantino used the theme song and plot elements from it in his epic *Kill Bill*. This brought worldwide attention to the original manga, and Kamimura's work was translated into English in 2005 by Dark Horse publishers. Translations of Kamimura's other works followed. In 2009, Marvel's *Daredevil* franchise created a character, Lady Bullseye, as a tribute to Lady Snowblood.

kiroku higaki

(b.1940 Yamaguchi-ken, Japan)

Loin du Vietnam was a collaborative documentary between six French New Wave filmmakers opposed to the Vietnam War: Jean-Luc Godard, William Klein, Joris Ivens, Agnès Varda, Claude Lelouch and Alain Resnais. Documentarian Chris Marker took their footage and edited it into a whole, complete with his own damning voiceover. Kiroku Higaki's sparingly stark design for the Japanese release was a reflection of the new wave of poster artists that ATG encouraged to take a fresh approach to film promotion.

Higaki worked on a number of posters for ATG, including Jean-Luc Godard's *Alphaville*. Higaki worked for Toho-Towa (who were financial backers of ATG), eventually leaving the studio to establish his own firm, Office 63.

Loin du Vietnam (1967), Japanese one sheet

Alphaville (1965), Japanese one sheet

kiyoshi awazu

(1929 Tokyo, Japan—2009 Kawasaki, Japan)

The self-taught artist and designer Kiyoshi Awazu was singularly talented, his genius having an extraordinary impact on post-war graphic design in Japan. Awazu first came to attention for his award-winning poster for *Give Back Our Sea* at the Japan Advertising Exhibition in 1955—beginning a lifelong association with political advocacy and social causes. In 1958 he won first prize at the World Film Poster Competition in France and a year later, he opened the Awazu Design Institute (later the Awazu Design Room). In 1970 he won a Silver Medal and special mention at the Warsaw International Poster Biennale.

Already well established as a leader in the field of poster design, Awazu's versatility saw him expand into urban design, exhibition design, writing, and art direction for theatre and film—winning an award for his art direction of the *Shinjû: Ten no amijima/Double Suicide* (1969). In 1990 Awazu was awarded a Medal with Purple Ribbon by the Japanese government as a person of outstanding artistic merit. His works are held in the permanent collections of MoMA in New York, the Museum of Modern Art in Toyama and at the Stedelijk Museum in Amsterdam.

Awazu actively rebelled against the reigning doctrine of Japanese modernism and instead his work was complex and expressive, chaotic and vibrantly colourful. Folklore, history and a dialogue between the rural and urban space were common threads in his paintings. In Japan, only a handful of graphic designers engaged in the film poster as an artistic medium. Three of Awazu's most well-known film posters—Godard's *Le Vent d'est*, *Week-end* and *La Chinoise*—unusually took a wholly photographic approach yet they remain recognizably Awazu through the multiple elements at play within each design and his bright use of colour.

La Chinoise (1967), Japanese one sheet

lajos görög

(1927 Budapest, Hungary—1995 Budapest, Hungary)

Hungarian artist Lajos Görög's interpretation of *Orfeu Negro* uses a dense red and blue to reflect the richness of the film's colourful scenes. His use of the negative black space and facial expression, however, darken the poster's whole effect and serves to emphasise the ominous presence of death stalking the star-crossed lovers.

Görög studied at the University of Applied Arts in Budapest and at the University of Fine Arts under the celebrated poster artist György Konecsni. Görög graduated in the early 1950s and was part of the new wave of Hungarian graphic artists that emerged at this time. He was a member of the influential Papp Group from 1963 and had several exhibitions of his work. He won the 1965 Munkácsy Prize and Best Poster of the Year awards four times between 1958 and 1973. Görög often worked in a restrained palette of just two or three colours, with a naïve boldness to his designs. In addition to *Orfeu Negro*, two of his most recognised posters are for *Rocco and his Brothers* (1960) and *8½* (1963).

Orfeu Negro (1959), Hungarian one sheet

liliana baczewska

(b.1931 Warsaw, Poland)

Les Sept péchés capitaux was a portmanteau film showcasing the work of a number of French New Wave directors, each of whom directed different chapters with different casts. The seven segments were dedicated to the seven deadly sins and the directors involved were Philippe de Broca, Claude Chabrol, Jacques Demy, Sylvain Dhomme, Max Douy, Jean-Luc Godard, Eugène Ionesco,

Edouard Molinaro and Roger Vadim.

Liliana Baczewska's painting of a smiling devil to incorporate all seven shorts was an appropriate and witty choice, characteristic of Baczewska's imaginative approach. One of the few female artists of the Polish Poster School, Baczewska graduated from the Warsaw Academy of Fine Arts in 1956. Less than a year later, she won the distinguished Trepkowski

Award for one of her posters, *July 22*. She went on to create a number of well-known film posters, including *Darling* (1965) and *101 Dalmations* (1967), and has held exhibitions of her work in Berlin, Beirut and Warsaw, among others.

Les Sept péchés capitaux (1962), Polish one sheet

maciej hibner

(b.1931 Warsaw, Poland)

Maciej Hibner had a fascination with the human head and it appears as a recurring motif in his work, dominating the space as with his poster for *Lola*. He is also renowned for his exquisite colour palette. The dense greens and blues in his poster for *Pickpocket*—an unusually literal interpretation of a scene for Poland—were enriched by his block use of black and the white highlights in the face and hands of the pickpocket.

Hibner graduated from the Warsaw Academy of Fine Arts in 1955 and was a key player in establishing the new aesthetic of the Polish poster school with his designs for film, theatre and travel. His work is greatly admired and he has won several awards. Exhibitions of his work have been held worldwide, including London, Paris and Rome.

Lola (1961), Polish one sheet

Pickpocket (1959), Polish one sheet

maciej żbikowski

(b.1935 Przasnysz, Poland)

Yoyo (1965), Polish one sheet

Inspired by cartoonish Pop Art and psychedelic artists like Peter Max, Polish artist Maciej Żbikowski created a large body of posters for some of the most popular films of the 1960s and 1970s, including *The Graduate* (1967), *Where Eagles Dare* (1968) and *Sabrina* (1954, for 1967 release). He also created artwork for the New Wave films *Baisers volés* and *Yoyo*.

Żbikowski had spent time studying in Prague before studying graphics at the Warsaw Academy of Fine Arts, where he graduated in 1960. In addition to his successful career as a poster artist, he also illustrated for a number of weekly satirical magazines such as *Szpilki* and *Polska* and worked in animation. He has exhibited internationally in countries that include Russia, Germany and China.

Yoyo (1965), Polish special sheet

marcello colizzi

(b.1929 Rome, Italy)

La Mariée était en noir (1968), Italian lobby sheet (detail)

Marcello Colizzi grew up in a household surrounded by illustration. His father, Gioacchino 'Attalo' Colizzi, was one of the leading satirical and humour cartoonists of his day, working for newspapers like *Marc-Aurelio* and *Paese Sera*. Marcello's own passion for art led him to study at the Accademia delle Belle Arti in Rome and after graduation, he focussed on film poster art, learning his craft in the studio of poster artist extraordinaire Ercole Brini. Colizzi created numerous posters for both American films like *The Man Who Shot Liberty Valance* (1962) and *Zulu* (1964) and Italian films like Mario Bava's *Blood and Lace* (1971). He is also known for his circus posters and for his book illustrations for children's fairytales. Colizzi retired from commercial illustration in the 1980s and moved to Lavinio, where he still lives.

masakatsu ogasawara

(b.1942 Tokyo, Japan)

Masakatsu Ogasawara graduated from the prestigious Musashino Art University in the early 1960s and worked as a film poster designer for over 40 years. He frequently worked for Toho/Towa distribution company, and through Toho's links to ATG, also had the opportunity to take a more graphically bold approach to design for ATG's releases. His poster for *Le Feu follet* keeps to the Japanese photographic tradition but with a much more deliberate approach, isolating the photographs against a strong black background to give them greater impact. The black and white contrasting with the colourful typography also makes the poster's impact very arresting.

Le Feu follet (1963), Japanese one sheet

maria syska

(dates and information unknown)

La Mariée était en noir (1968), Polish one sheet

milena kadlecová

(dates and information unknown)

L'Amour à vingt ans (1962), Czechoslovakian one sheet

milton glaser

(b.1929, New York, USA)

A giant in his field, Milton Glaser revolutionised post-war graphic design in the twentieth century. He brought a fierce intelligence and playfulness to his craft, creating works of extraordinary visual impact. His designs have become part of the cultural lexicon of our time and include the I [heart] NY logo, produced pro-bono in 1977 for the state of New York; Bob Dylan's profile in silhouette with psychedelic hair for his *Greatest Hits* album in 1966 and the World Health Organization's official Aids awareness poster in 1987 of a skull splitting a heart in two.

Glaser studied at the Cooper Union Art School in New York, followed by a year in Italy on a Fulbright scholarship. On his return to the States, he co-founded Push Pin Studios with fellow Cooper Union graduates. Push Pin took a groundbreaking approach to graphic design, establishing itself as a pioneering, cutting-edge creative force. Such was their international renown that in 1970, they became the first American studio to have an exhibition at the Louvre's Musée des Arts Décoratifs in Paris, which then toured worldwide.

In 1968, Glaser co-founded *New York* magazine with Clay Felker, defining its look and graphic approach as president and design director until 1977. In the mid-1970s, Glaser set up his own company, Milton Glaser, Inc. to expand his design into a more multidisciplinary approach that included not only magazine, newspaper and poster design but also exhibition, restaurant, supermarket and interior design, packaging and corporate identity. Of his company's versatility, he has commented that, 'We have a varied palate. I have always been interested in being a design generalist. I try not to be too narrow in scope and we do a lot of different things.'

Glaser has had one man shows at MoMA in New York and Centre Pompidou in Paris. He received the lifetime achievement award from Cooper Hewitt Smithsonian Design Museum in 2004 and the Fulbright Association in 2011. In 2009 he became the first graphic designer to receive the National Medal of the Arts award. Glaser lectures at the Cooper Union and the School of Visual Arts in New York.

Glaser has created over 500 posters—many award-winning and iconic—although is rather critical of his work for client Personality Posters, Inc. for the *La Guerre est finie* screening at 5th Avenue Cinema in New York: 'The drawing of the stylization of the hand seems extremely clumsy to me in terms of the way I conceptualize a hand now. . . . I don't think that was a particularly good poster . . . sometimes a good drawing can be a mediocre poster, which is to say it doesn't inform you perhaps enough about the spirit of the film or give you an adequate reason to go see it.'

La Guerre Est Finie
Yves Montand/Ingrid Thulin/Directed by Alain Resnais
5th Avenue Cinema at 12th Street

La Guerre est finie (1966), American special sheet for 5th Avenue Cinema

miroslav vystrčil

(1924 Brno, Czechoslovakia—2015 Prague, Czech Republic)

The Czechoslovakian poster for *Les Parapluies de Cherbourg* was designed by the celebrated sculptor Miroslav Vystrčil. Vystrčil employed themes common to the new wave of Eastern European graphic designers—bold colour blocking, photography and graphics, clean lines, with every piece of necessary information shrewdly incorporated into the design. One of the most pleasing touches in this poster is the credits: instead of their usual relegation to the bottom of the poster they become an essential part of the design, hitting the umbrella as raindrops.

Although Vystrčil designed a number of notable film posters it is for his sculpture that he is most acclaimed and remembered. He was a core member of the May 57 group of artists, exhibiting his plaster sculptures in their first three exhibitions. By the 1960s, he had begun working in metal, the material he would favour for the rest of his career. He earned a reputation as a leading talent in his field and exhibited in several group and solo exhibitions. Retrospectives of his work were held in the Czech towns of Cheb in 2017 and Náchod in 2019.

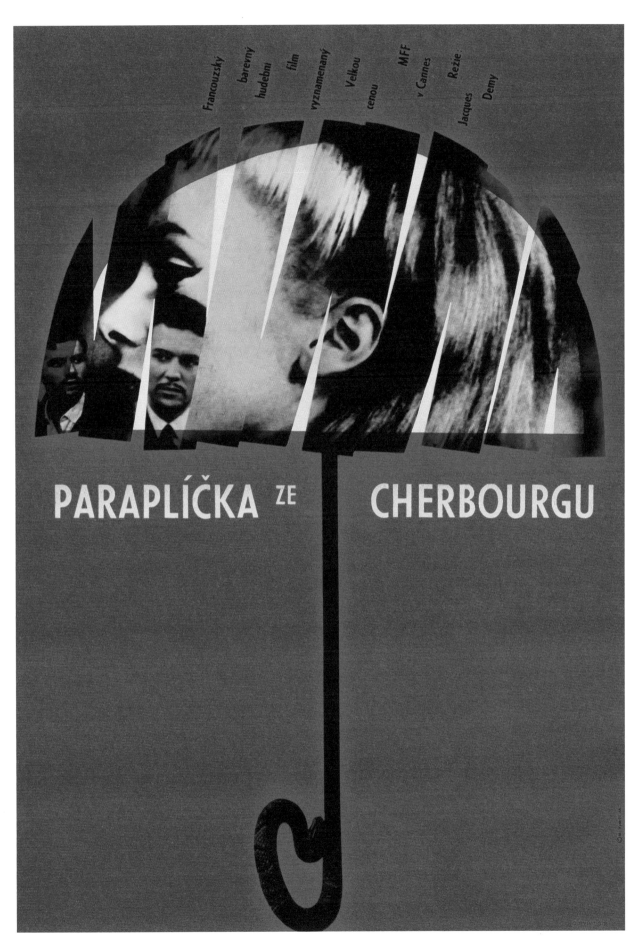

Les Parapluies de Cherbourg (1962), Czechoslovakian one sheet

nándor szilvásy

(1927 Makó, Hungary—2011 Budapest, Hungary)

Yoyo (1965), Hungarian one sheet

An important influence on Hungarian graphic design in the second half of the twentieth century, Nándor Szilvásy had a long and varied career in his field. He graduated from the College of Applied Arts in 1949 and the College of Fine Arts in 1952. During the 1950s, Szilvásy's main focus was on children's book illustration and in the 1960s he worked more as a poster artist. He embraced a humorous, often surreal approach, employing bold childlike brushstrokes and bright graphics. Szilvásy also frequently worked with collage and photography. Like many artists in Eastern Europe, the typography was a playful and integral part of his designs. In 1962, Szilvásy won the Munkácsy Prize and in 1978 the Meritorious Artist Award. From 1963, he was a member of the Papp Group of artists. Between 1963 and 1983 he led Kontakt Design Studio and from 2000 he was art director of *New Horizon* magazine. From 2004 to 2011 he was a member of the Hungarian Poster Association.

Yoyo (1965), Hungarian unused artwork

paris pullman cinema

The Paris Pullman was an arthouse cinema in the borough of Kensington and Chelsea in London. In 1967, it was taken over by film enthusiast and producer Charles Cooper of Contemporary Films with his wife Kitty. Contemporary had been an important player in the distribution of arthouse feature films, shorts and documentaries from around the world since it was established in the early 1950s. The Coopers were the first to introduce British audiences to films by directors such as Ingmar Bergman, Satyajit Ray, Bernardo Bertolucci, Werner Herzog, Jean Renoir, Sergei Eisenstein, and many films of the French New Wave. Cooper's politics also informed the films Contemporary distributed. *Loin du Vietnam* was very much in a similar political vein to left-wing films such as Frederic Rossif's *To Die in Madrid*, about the Spanish Civil War, and also *March to Aldermaston*, a documentary about the first anti-nuclear march, that Contemporary also helped to make. With their acquisition of the Paris Pullman and also the Phoenix in East Finchley in London and the Phoenix in Oxford, the Coopers now had an avenue to screen their catalogue of films. Contemporary employed uncredited, in-house artists to design the posters for the Paris Pullman. The poster tagline reflected the film's condemnation of the conflict and was also a cry to action.

PARIS PULLMAN
Cinema
Drayton Gardens, S.W. 10
FRE 5898
Buses: 14 & 30
Tubes: Gloucester Rd & South Kensington.

'Far from Vietnam'

The war of the rich
against the poor

7000 miles away - or
much, much closer ?

A film by:

JEAN LUC GODARD: ("Une Femme Mariêe")
AGNES VARDA: ("Le Bonheur")
ALAIN RESNAIS: ("Hiroshima Mon Amour")
CLAUDE LELOUCH: ("Un Homme et Une Femme")
& MICHELE RAY, WILLIAM KLEIN, JORIS IVENS,
CHRIS MARKER.

A Contemporary Films release

Loin du Vietnam (1967) British special sheet for London's Paris Pullman Cinema

peter strausfeld

(1910 Cologne, Germany — 1980 Great Britain)

Peter Strausfeld was one of Britain's most important post-war poster designers. Born in Germany, Strausfeld was openly opposed to the Nazis and came to Brighton in Britain with the outbreak of the Second World War. Interned on the Isle of Man in 1940-41, he developed a friendship with a fellow internee, the Austrian film producer George Hoellering. After the war, Hoellering became the director of the Academy Cinema on London's Oxford Street — the city's leading arthouse cinema. Hoellering commissioned Strausfeld to create the posters for the cinema's releases, to be displayed across the London underground network. For over 30 years from 1947 to 1980, Strausfeld designed over 300 posters for the picture house. Featuring a single scene and a single colour, he produced his posters using his trademark traditional woodcut technique. His design for *Murder in the Cathedral* won the prize for best art direction at the Venice Film Festival in 1951. Strausfeld also illustrated for the prestigious Folio Society, and lectured in the graphics department of Brighton College of Art (later Brighton Polytechnic) from 1959 to his death in 1980.

À bout de souffle (1960), artist's proof for British quad sheet

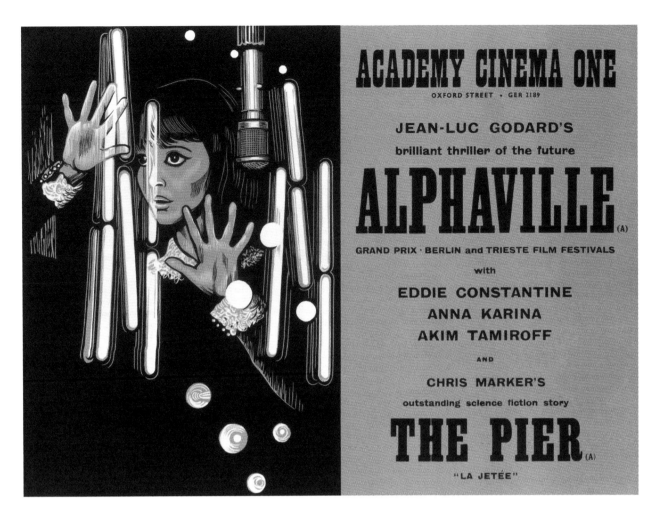

Alphaville (1965), British quad sheet

pierre étaix

(1928 Roanne, France—2016 Paris, France)

François Truffaut said of Jacques Tati that like Robert Bresson, he 'invents cinema as he makes a film; he rejects anyone else's structures'. Tati used slapstick and the absurd to subtly critique society.

Pierre Étaix was a renowned artist, designer, filmmaker and clown. A fan of the intelligent slapstick comedy of the silent screen, Étaix was frequently called 'the French Buster Keaton'. He moved to Paris from the Loire region in his mid-twenties and worked as an illustrator while also performing in cabaret and as a circus clown with the celebrated Nino Fabri. In 1954, a chance meeting with Jacques Tati resulted in Étaix collaborating on Tati's *tour-de-force*, *Mon Oncle*, as assistant director, gagman and designer. Étaix was also responsible for the striking French poster campaign for the film. The minimal graphics and bold colour scheme was very modern for the time—not only in France but also worldwide—and has since become one of the most famous posters of the 1950s. Étaix's work on *Mon Oncle* gave him a taste for filmmaking and in 1961 he made his first short film, *Out*. This was followed two years later by *Happy Birthday*, which won him an Academy Award for Best Short Film. Between 1963 and 1970, he made five feature films, including the New Wave *Le Soupirant* (1962) and *Yoyo* (1964). In 1973, he formed the National Circus School in France with his wife Annie Fratellini, and the couple also toured as a clowning double-act.

Mon Oncle (1958), French one sheet

pino milas

(dates unknown)

Pino Migliazzo (known as Pino Milas) was an art director at the advertising agency Agens in Argentina. The exclusive agency had originally been set up as the in-house department for renowned industrial manufacturing company Siam Di Tella, with the advertising department under the leadership of Frank Memelsdorff and the architect Carlos Méndez Mosquera. They fostered young, fresh talent in design and art. In addition to Pino Milas, other names that worked for Agens that went on to very successful careers include architecture student Guillermo González Ruiz and artists Pérez Celis, Ronald Shakespear, Rómulo Macció and América Sánchez. From the mid 1960s, Agens was also doing corporate and advertising work for outside clients, including designing a small number of film posters, such as this striking design by Milas for *Alphaville*.

Alphaville (1965), Argentinian one sheet

raymond gid

(1905 Paris, France—2000 Paris, France)

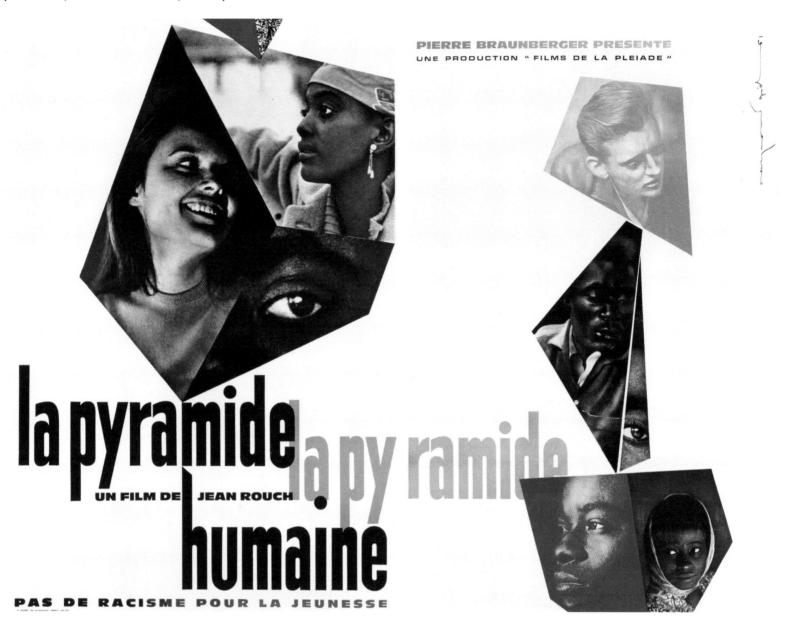

La Pyramide humaine (1961), French horizontal or vertical two sheet

Raymond Gid was a groundbreaking French graphic designer and typographer. His style was very free and conceptual and he had a singular ability to evoke an atmosphere through simple lines on a clean white or black background. His influence on the development of posters as an art form in the twentieth century has been significant.

Gid studied architecture at the École des Beaux Arts in Paris. He began designing advertising posters in 1926 for clients including Vermouth and Cinzano. Later years would also see him create posters for Bally Shoes, Amnesty International, Tour de France and many more. In 1930, Gid met Guy Lévis Mano, renowned publisher of illustrated editions of surrealist writers. Through Mano, Gid published his first book and then in the mid 1930s, Gid established his own publishing house, Éditions O.E.T., creating typography and illustrations for photographic books by Pierre Jahan, Ylla, Ergy Landau and others, and also illustrating well-known liturgical texts.

Vampyr was the first film poster Gid designed in 1932. He went on to create several of the most innovative, non-conformist French film posters of the twentieth century, including Melville's *Le Silence de la Mer* (1949) and Clouzot's *Les Diaboliques* (1955). Gid won numerous awards for his work, including the gold medal for posters at the International Exhibition of Paris in 1937, the National Poster Award in 1976 and 1979 and the Maximilien Vox Prize in 1984.

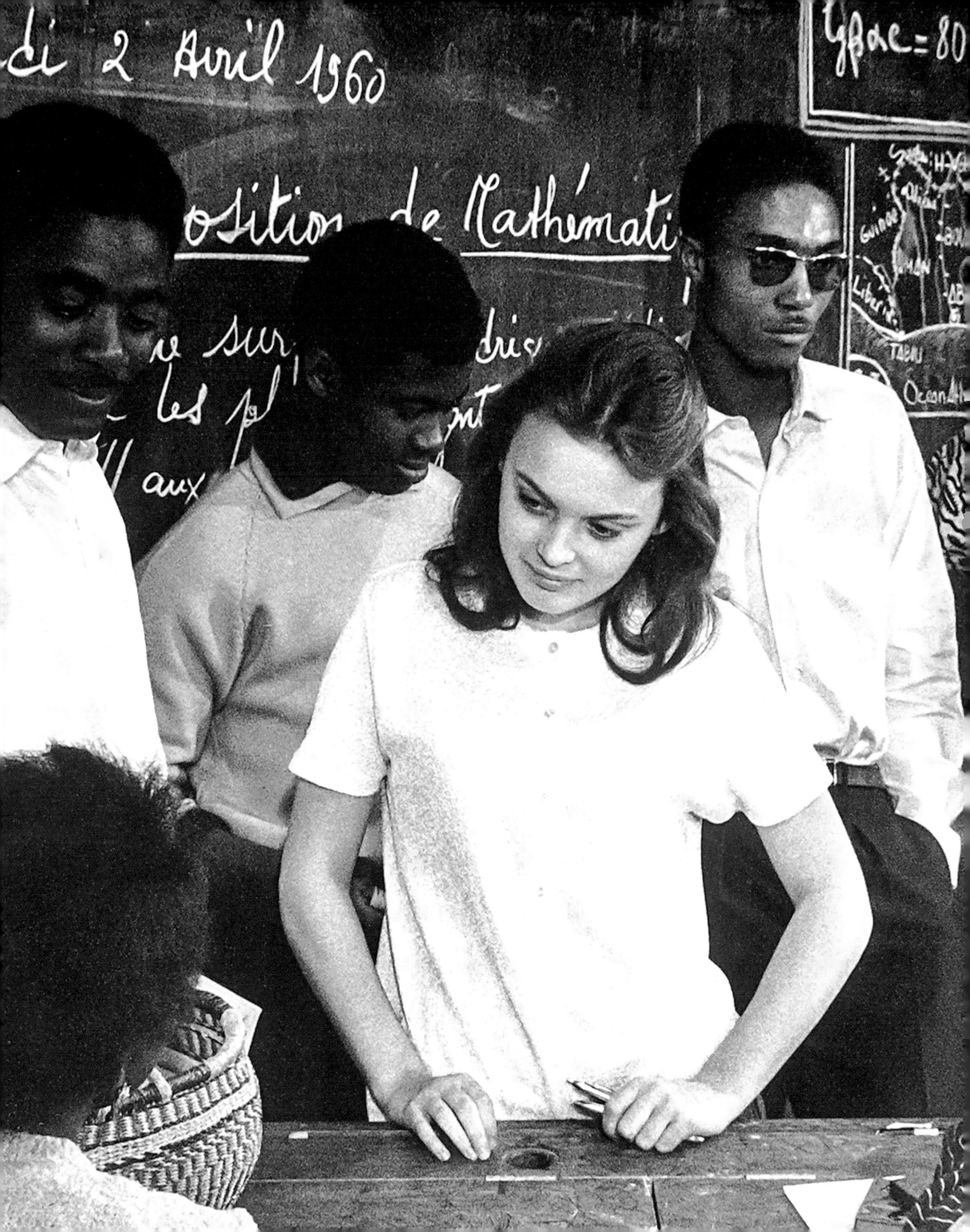
2 Avril 1960
osition de Mathémati
aux

Léon Morin, prêtre (1961), French mini sheet

rené ferracci

(1927 Paris, France—1982, France)

One of the most prolific poster designers of the twentieth century, René Ferracci created more than 3000 posters during his 40-year career, including several designs for the French New Wave.

Studying at the Estienne School in Paris under the painter and engraver René Cottet, Ferracci learned *intaglio* engraving, a technique in which a design or type is engraved during the printing process. Upon graduation he designed his first posters for a theatre agency, and also designed perfume bottles for Nina Ricci. In 1949, after his military service, he began working at MGM as head of advertising. In

1952, at just 25 years old, he became the artistic director of Filmsonor-Cinedis. At the weekend he also created work for other studios including Fox and Paramount. When Cinedis closed in 1963, he continued to work as a freelance artistic director for the top studios in France.

Ferracci was incredibly versatile and embraced new techniques in printing. He brought a tradition of painting and drawing to film poster design while combining it with modern innovations in the photographic approach. Attesting to his versatility are posters that range from the striking black and white portrait of Jeanne Moreau for Truffaut's *La Mariée était*

en noir to the exceptional collage for Godard's *Deux ou trois choses que je sais d'elle*. The use of photography in his posters for the films of the French New Wave was a particularly fitting reflection of the new reality that the movement sought to bring to cinema. Ferracci also had the rare talent of knowing which artists to bring into his creative process on specific projects. Frequent collaborators included the movie poster artists Yves Thos and Christian Broutin *(see p.66)*. Ferracci died of a heart attack in 1982 and was awarded the Cesar of Honor for his outstanding work in movie posters posthumously in 1986.

Le Feu follet (1963), French half sheet

Made in USA (1966), French one sheet

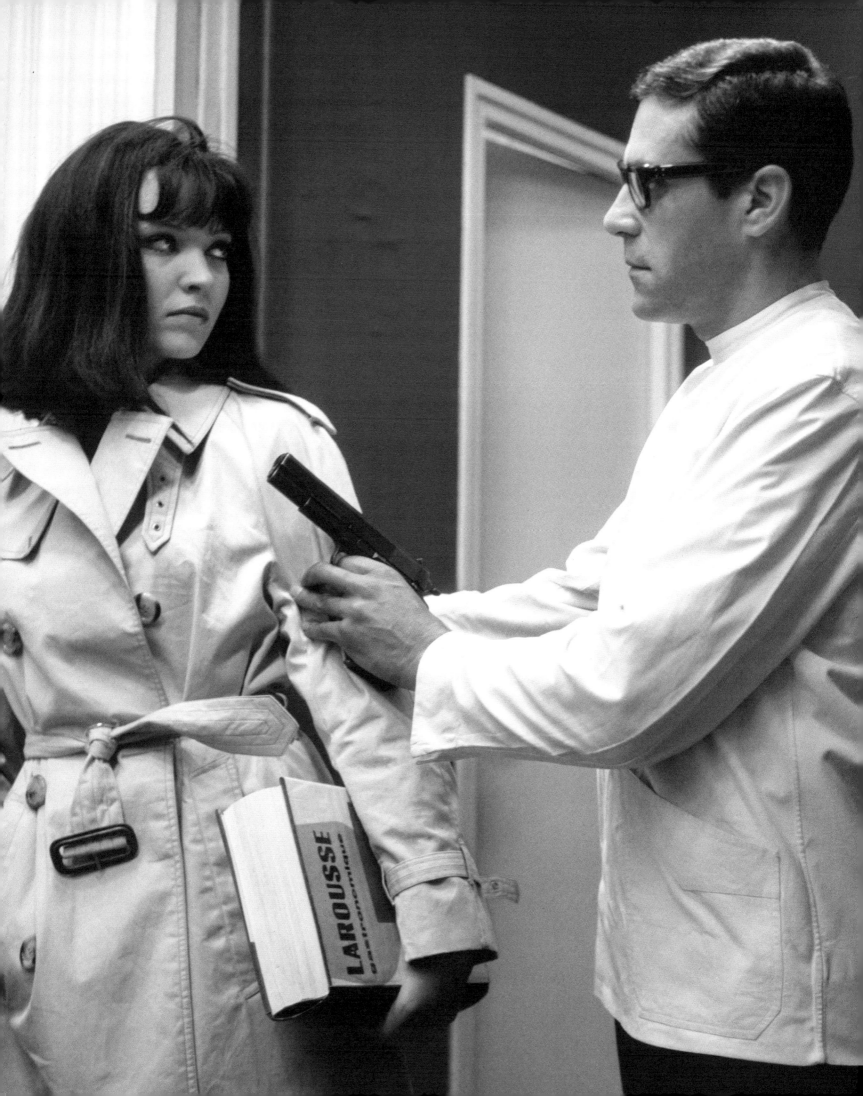

Le Samouraï (1967), French one sheet

Pierrot le Fou (1965), French one sheet

Trans-Europ-Express (1966), French one sheet

(Top) *La Mariée était en noir* (1968), French original artwork and one sheet; (bottom) *La Chinoise* (1967), production still and French one sheet

Deux ou trois choses que je sais d'elle (1967), French one sheet

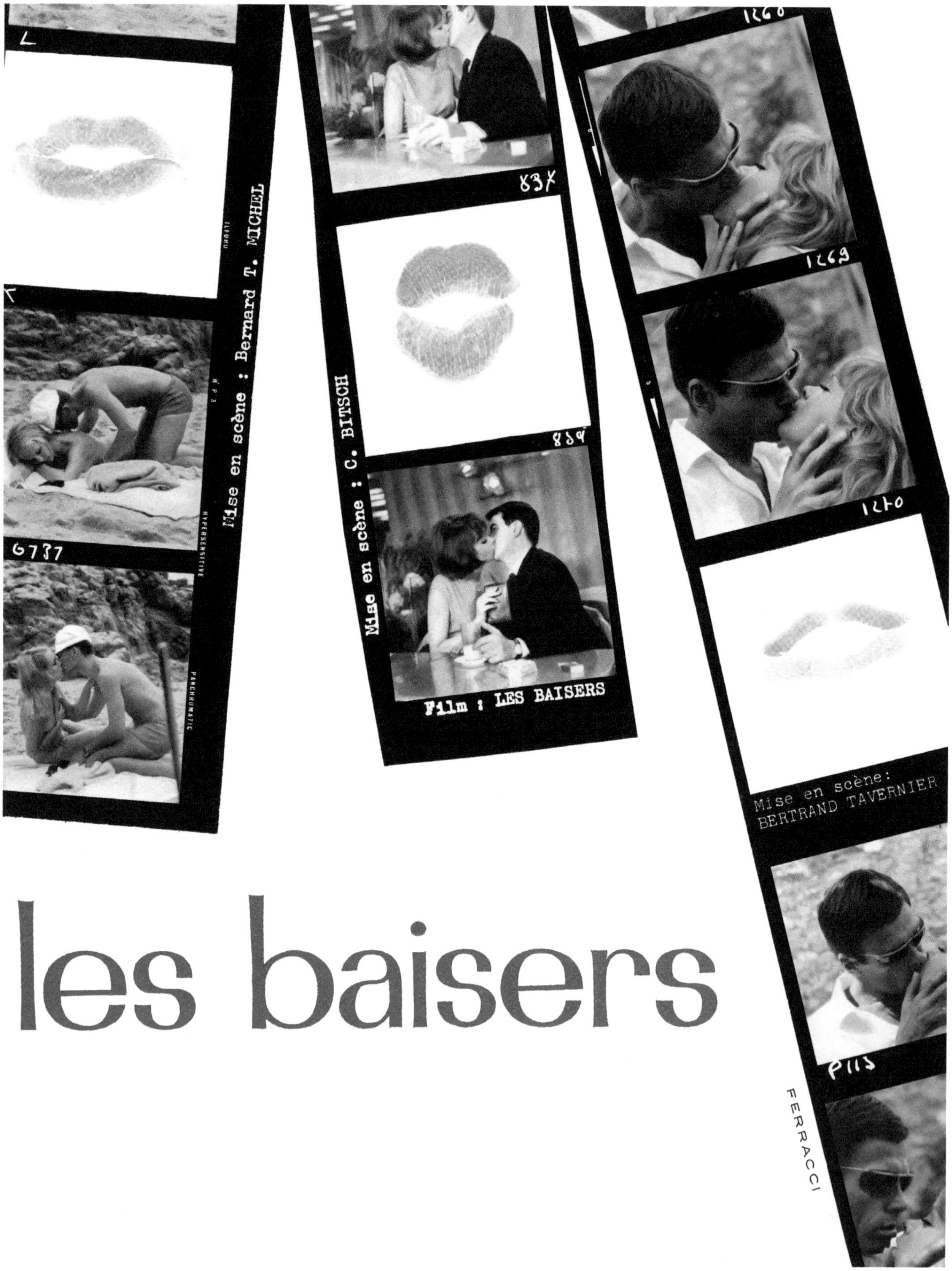
Mise en scène : Bernard T. MICHEL
Mise en scène : C. BITSCH
Film : LES BAISERS
Mise en scène:
BERTRAND TAVERNIER
les baisers
FERRACCI

Les Baisers **(1963), French tearsheet**

rené péron

(1904 France — 1972)

Et Dieu . . . créa la femme was the film that turned Brigitte Bardot into a worldwide star and established her perennial sex goddess image. Bardot's sultry turn was made even more exaggerated and scandalous by artist René Péron removing her clothes for the French poster.

Péron was renowned as a master of traditional French poster art and his eye-catching designs displayed a preference for strong and contrasting colours, often with a portrait of the stars turned slightly in profile. One of his earliest posters was for *King Kong* in 1933 and other notable works include *Suspicion* (1941), *The Stranger* (1946) and *Tokyo Joe (1949).* He created thousands of posters between the 1930s and 1960s before developing a second career in his later years as an illustrator of children's books.

Et Dieu . . . créa la femme (1956), French one panel

rolf goetze

(1921 Berlin, Germany—1988 Celle, Germany)

Pierrot le Fou (1965), German horizontal one sheet

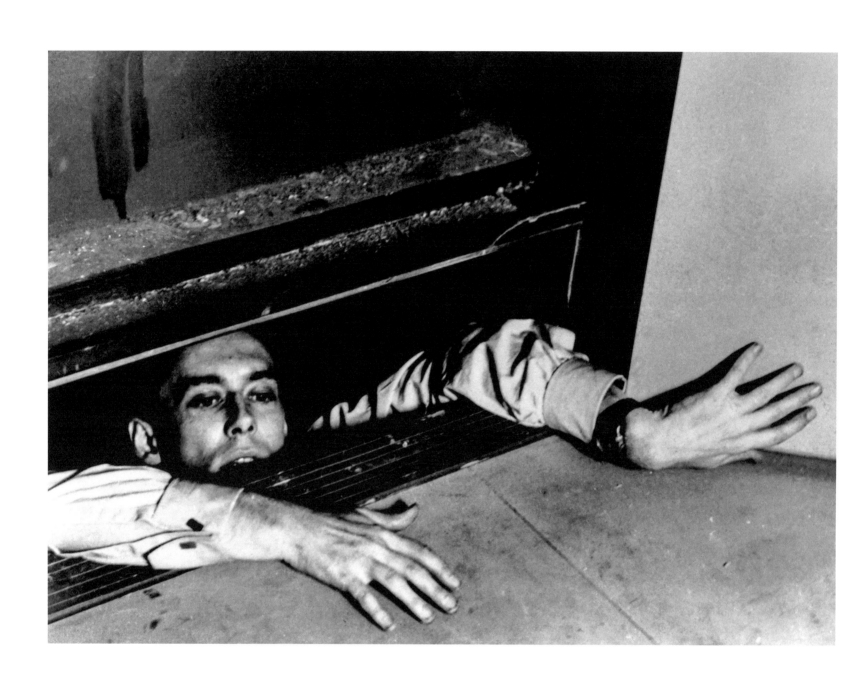

Ascenseur pour l'échafaud (1958), German one sheet

sandro symeoni

(1928 Ferrara, Italy—2007 Rome, Italy)

Sandro Symeoni studied art in Ferrara in Italy and began working as a caricaturist for local newspapers. In the 1950s, he moved to Rome to design film posters, gaining a formidable reputation as one of the best in the business. Over the course of his long career, he designed thousands of posters for both Italian and American films, including *Vertigo* (1958), *La Dolce Vita* (1960) and *A Fistful Of Dollars* (1964). He often chose to depict an intense moment or a scene heavy with emotional resonance, which is true of his posters for both *Ascenseur pour l'échafaud* and *Lola*.

ANOUK AIMÉE
MARC MICHEL
in

FranScope

DONNA DI VITA
(LOLA)

JACQUES HARDEN · ALAN SCOTT · MARGO LION · CARLO NELL · ISABELLA LUNGHINI

E CON **ELINA LABOURDETTE**   UN FILM DI **JACQUES DEMY**

Lola (1961), Italian two sheet

shunji sakai

(dates and information unknown)

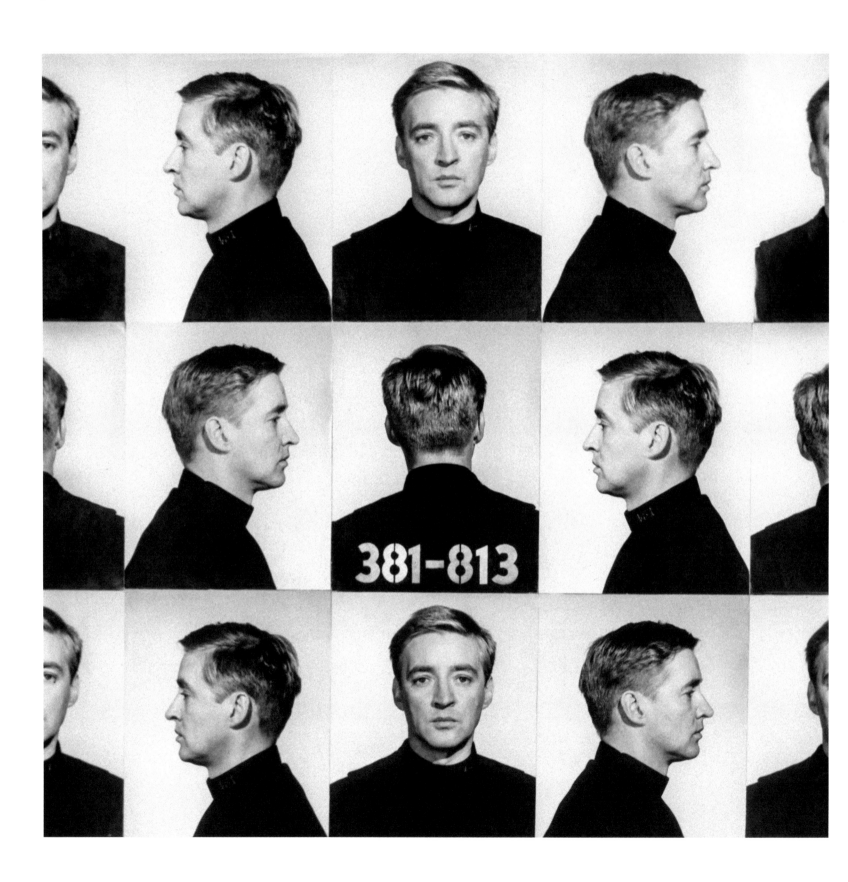

Fahrenheit 451 (1966), Japanese one panel

silvano campeggi (nano)

(1923, Florence, Italy—2018 Florence, Italy)

Silvano Campeggi had been exposed to the world of print and design at a young age through his father, a printer and typesetter. He went on to attend art school and study painting in Florence. During the Second World War, Campeggi was hired by the American Red Cross to paint the portraits of American soldiers before they returned home. After the war, he moved to Rome to look for work and met the celebrated poster artist Luigi Martinati, who encouraged

the young Campeggi to turn his talents to the cinematographic arts. His fresh talent attracted MGM studio, for whom he created the poster for *Gone With the Wind*. More work for MGM and other major studios followed and he developed a reputation as one of the most talented poster artists of his generation. He ultimately created over 3000 posters for films including *Casablanca* (1942, for the 1960s re-release), *Breakfast at Tiffany's* (1961) and *Cat on a Hot Tin Roof* (1958,

for the 1966 re-release). He was renowned for his portraits of A-list stars, which dominated the poster. He painted many of the greatest actors of the day including Audrey Hepburn, Marlon Brando, Humphrey Bogart, Rita Hayworth and Marilyn Monroe. Campeggi often signed his work with his family nickname 'Nano'.

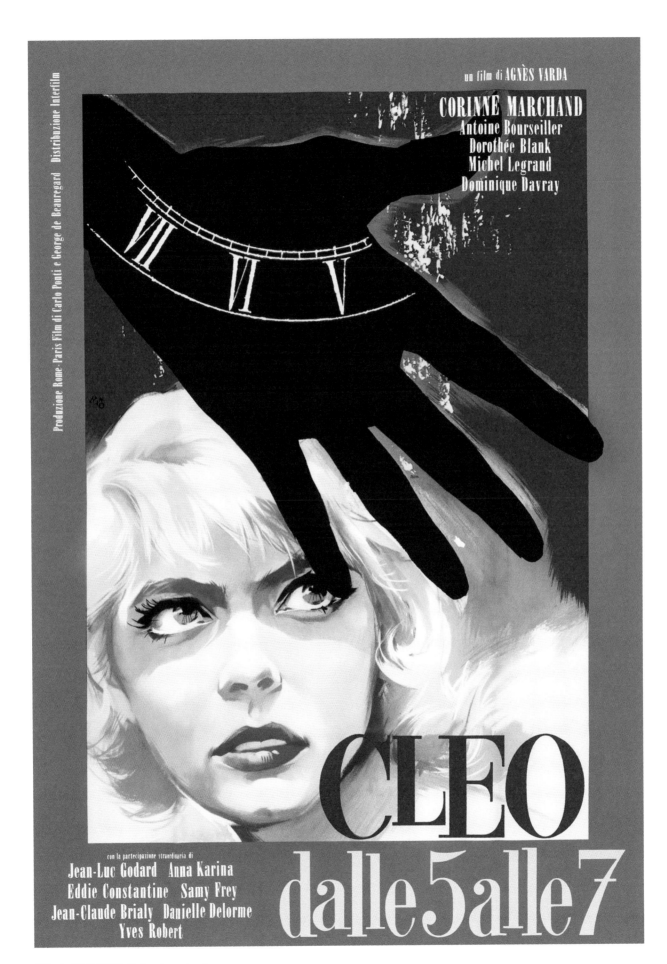

Cléo de 5 à 7 (1962), Italian four sheet

stanisław zagórski

(b.1933 Warsaw, Poland)

One of the co-founders of the Polish poster school, Stanisław Zagórski was also one of the first Polish graphic designers to forge a successful career in the United States. After graduating from the Academy of Fine Arts in Warsaw, he designed a number of film posters, including *Hiroshima, mon amour*. In the early 1960s, he moved to America, taking his bold modern ideas to the East Coast where he worked in advertising, designing posters and also book covers for the biggest names in publishing. In 1964 he began designing album covers for Atlantic Records and Columbia Records, including albums for Aretha Franklin, Miles Davis, The Velvet Underground and Cher, among others. Zagórski is also Professor Emeritus at the esteemed Tyler School of Art at Temple University in Philadelphia.

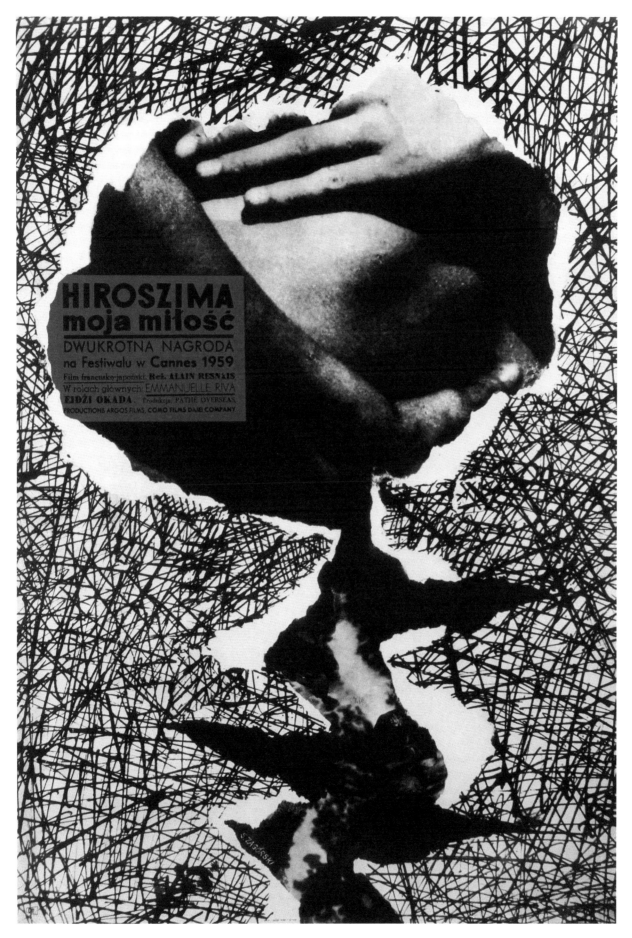

Hiroshima, mon amour (1960), Polish one sheet

tab design studio

LE PETIT SOLDAT

監督・脚本・脚色・台詞■ジャン＝リュック・ゴダール

小さな兵隊

強迫！拷問！暗殺！ジュネーヴに激突する二つの諜報機関、隠謀にまきこまれた一人の男、ブルーノ

アルジェリア戦争批判のかどで
上映禁止となった
ゴダールの問題作！

アンナ・カリーナ
ミジェル・シュボール
ラズロ・サボ

撮影■ラウール・クタール
音楽■モーリス・ルルウ

LA SOCIÉTE NOUVELLE
DE CINEMATOGRAPHIE

ANNA KARINA
MICHE SUBOR

dans un film de

JEAN-LUC GODARD

日本A・T・G配給

フランス映画社

Le Petit Soldat (1963), Japanese one sheet

Hitler, connais pas (1963), Japanese one sheet

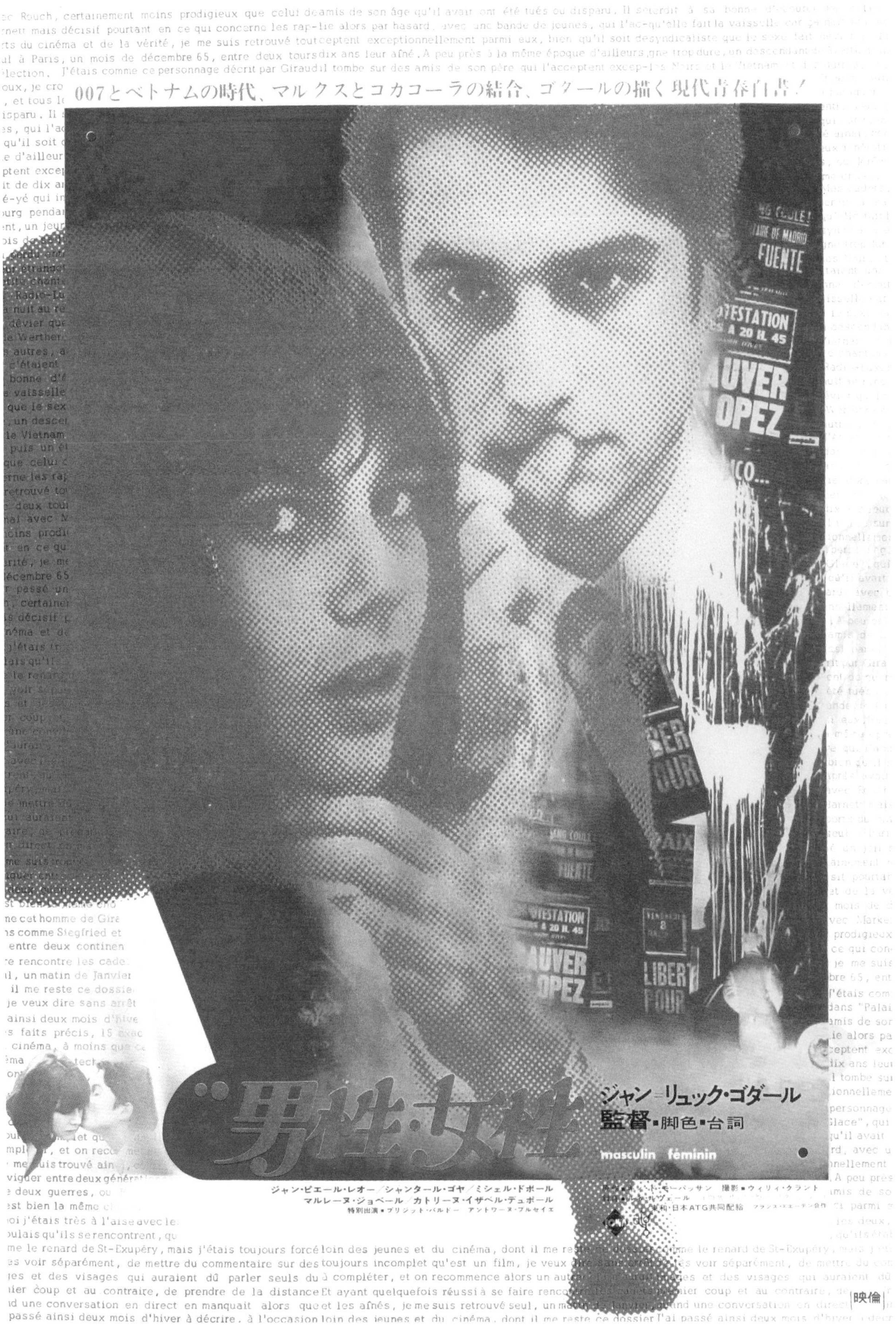

***Masculin Féminin* (1966), Japanese one sheet**

映倫

流行のメッカ パリ・ファッション界
そこから生まれでたモードの申し子
ポリー・マグー！
● 消費文明に鋭い諷刺を放つクラインの異色作！

ドロシー・マクコヴァン
ジャン・ロシュフォール
サミー・フレイ
フイリップ・ノワレ
グレイソン・ホール

監督■ウイリアム・クライン
脚本・脚色・台詞■ウイリアム・クライン
撮影■ジャン・ボフティ
装置■ベルナール・エヴァン
音楽■ミシェル・ルグラン
atg 日本A・T・G配給
〈フランス映画〉

Qui
êtes-vous
Polly
Maggoo

ポリー・マグーお前は誰だ

Realisateur ■ WILLIAM KLEIN
Scenario Adaptation Dialogues ■ WILLIAM KLEIN

DOROTHY MAC GOWAN
JEAN ROCHEFORT
SAMY FREY

Qui êtes-vous, Polly Maggoo? (1966), Japanese one sheet

tino avelli

(b.1938 Tripoli, Italy)

Tino Avelli attended art school in Catania. He also trained at the Academy of Fine Arts in Rome and studied the art of the nude at the French Academy in the city. He brought this talent for depicting the human form, especially women, to his work in the field of movie posters—as illustrated by his background collage in the poster for *Baisers volés*. Studying under the renowned poster artist Ercole Brini, Avelli learned how to combine his talent for illustration and watercolours with a graphic and commercially-minded approach. He created numerous film posters including *The Great Escape* (1963), *The Thomas Crown Affair* (1968) and *Il Decameron* (1971).

Avelli often used the colour red in his work for emphasis but never more so than in *Baisers volés*, which deliberately uses a blast of red and pink blocking to highlight Jean-Pierre Leaud's solitary figure in the centre of the poster. The flower, heart and recurring smiles signpost to the audience that this romantic comedy is one of the more light-hearted films of the French New Wave.

MAURICE RONET
w filmie francuskim
nagrodzonym   na MFF w Wenecji
BŁĘDNY   OGNIK
Reżyseria: LOUIS
MALLE

PRODUKCJA
NOUVELLES EDITIONS DE FILMS

Le Fe… …), Polish one sheet

vasil miovský

(b.1938 Prague, Czechoslovakia)

Vasil Miovský's arresting poster for *Le deuxième souffle*—featuring a wash of blood red over a photographic collage of Lino Ventura—effectively communicated the film-noir atmosphere of Jean-Pierre Melville's gangster masterpiece. Based on a novel by José Giovanni, Melville's intense thriller explored the complexities of the French criminal underworld. The film starred the inimitable Ventura at his most hard-boiled as the gangster Gustave 'Gu' Minda opposite the suave Paul Meurisse as Inspector Blot. Ventura and Meurisse both went on to work with Melville again on his French Resistance drama, *L'armée des ombres*, in 1969.

Le deuxième souffle (1966), Czechoslovakian one sheet

vladimír tesař

(1924 Prague, Czechoslovakia—2008 Prague, Czech Republic)

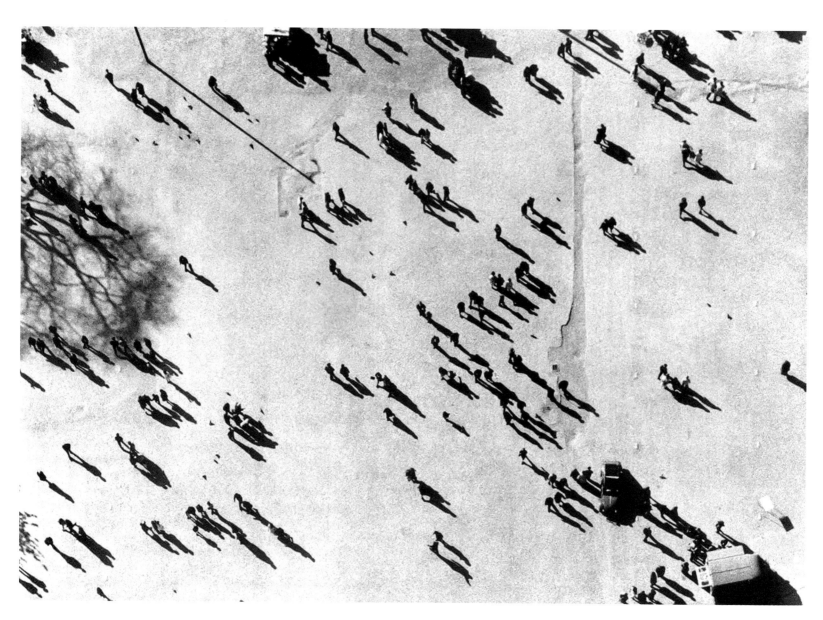

Chris Marker and Pierre Lhomme's *Le Joli Mai* was a profound portrait of everyday Paris; a montage of scenes featuring normal Parisians that also served as a comment on the wider societal struggles at the time. Notably, these included the impact of changes to the urban landscape on the city's inhabitants, and also reactions to Algeria's imminent independence and the end of the war.

Vladimír Tesař was responsible for the poster for the film's Czechoslovakian release. The naïve design features simple graphics, bold colour and photographic collage, which were common themes in Tesař's practice. The graphic designer, painter, typographer and scenographer had studied at the State Graphic School and the Academy of Fine Arts in Prague. He was a member of the influential

May 57 Group and Hollar Association of Czech Artists, taking part in group and individual shows. Tesař was also renowned for his work as a book illustrator, most famously for the 150th anniversary publication of Goethe's *Faust*. In 1963, he won the Czechoslovak Writer Award for Art Cooperation and the 1984 state Meritorious Artist title. His work is held in public and private collections worldwide.

Le Joli Mai (1963), Czechoslovakian one sheet

willy mucha

(1905 Warsaw, Poland—1995 Paris, France)

Willy Mucha was born in Warsaw and studied music and art in his native Poland, training with the Polish painter-engraver Ladislas Zkoczylas. He then travelled in Russia, Austria-Bohemia and Germany before moving to Caen in France. He fought in the Spanish Civil War and was part of the French Resistance during the Second World War. At the end of the war, he settled permanently in Collioure, the 'pearl' of the Vermillion Coast prized by artists for its light and picturesque beauty. It became the inspiration for most of his work for the next 50 years—in particular the panorama he viewed from his terrace, which looked out to the lighthouse and the sea. He once said that 'If my roots are not in the earth, they are in your sky, Collioure.' He also created the modern stained glass windows of the Argelès-Plage chapel in Argelès-sur-Mer and illustrated books.

As well as being a famous artist, Willy Mucha has also come to be known posthumously as a celebrated friend of artists. He was part of a strong artistic community and friends with everyone of cultural note, hosting them at his home from the late 1940s onwards. He asked all of his guests to contribute to a 'guest book' of sorts—a painting, a sketch or a written piece. His friends included Picasso, Miro, Chagall, Matisse, Dali, Man Ray, Cocteau, Joseph Kessel, Louis Aragon and René Barjavel, among others. Called the *Livre d'Or* or *Book of Gold and Light*, it has contributions from 98 of the most renowned artists of the twentieth century and is opened by Mucha's dedication that the book is 'for the glorificiation of Collioure, last place of free spirits, poets errant, painters thirsty for pure colour.' He bequeathed the book to the public on his death and it has since been included in a number of exhibitions worldwide and is considered an incredibly unique and valuable document.

Lux
Présente:

LE PRIX LOUIS DELLUC
La plus haute récompense Française du Cinéma

JEANNE MOREAU
et
MAURICE RONET

dans un Film réalisé par
LOUIS MALLE

Ascenseur pour l'échafaud

D'APRÈS LE ROMAN DE NOEL CALEF·ADAPTATION DE ROGER NIMIER ET LOUIS MALLE
DIALOGUE DE ROGER NIMIER
avec GEORGES POUJOULY·YORI BERTIN·JEAN WALL
et IVAN PETROVICH et FELIX MARTEN et LINO VENTURA
MUSIQUE DE MILES DAVIS
PRODUCTION NOUVELLES ÉDITIONS de FILMS·PRODUCTEUR DÉLÉGUÉ: JEAN THUILLIER

Ascenseur pour l'échafaud (1958), French one sheet, style B

waldemar świerzy

(1931 Katowice, Poland—2013 Warsaw, Poland)

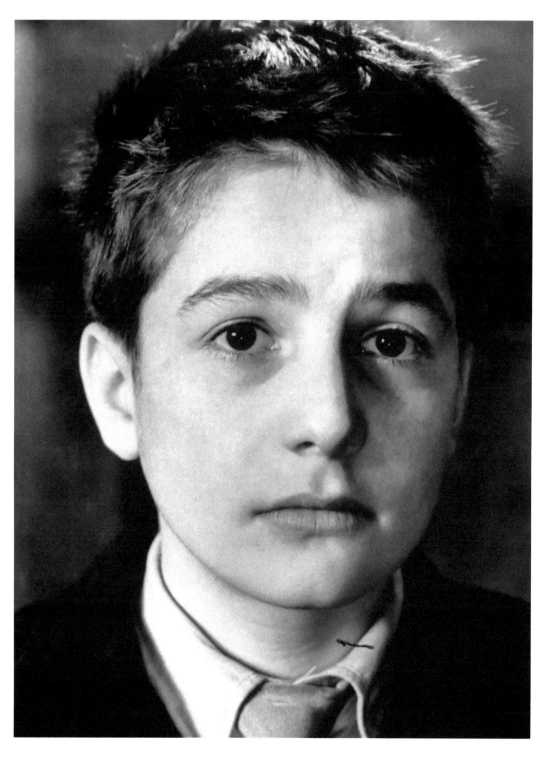

Waldemar Świerzy was one of the most important poster artists of post-war Poland. He began designing posters in the early 1950s after graduating from the Academy of Fine Arts in Krakow, producing a vast body of award-winning work. One of the most prolific of the Polish poster school, he created over 2500 posters. Świerzy was an extraordinarily gifted painter, adept in traditional techniques of pencil, gouache and watercolour yet he also understood the impact of clean, modern graphic design and new movements in photography, collage and Pop Art. He combined these multiple styles to powerful effect. He often made the head or face the focus of his design and consciously limited his palette of colours. In doing so, he intensified the psychological content and impact of his designs.

Świerzy's work has been exhibited in several solo exhibitions worldwide and some of his many awards include the 1959 Toulouse-Lautrec poster prize at the International Exhibition of Film Poster in Versailles and first prize at the Prix X Biennale in São Paulo in 1970. His celebrated works include posters for *Sunset Boulevard* (1957), *Midnight Cowboy* (1973) and *Apocalypse Now* (1979, for first Polish release 1981). From 1965, he was a professor at the Academy of Fine Arts in Poznań and from 1994 a professor at the Academy of Fine Arts in Warsaw.

REŻYSERIA: F. TRUFFAUT
NAGRODA — CANNES 1959

SZEROKOEKRANOWY FILM PRODUKCJI FRANCUSKIEJ (CAROSSE)
W ROLACH GŁÓWNYCH: JEAN-PIERRE LEAUD PATRICK AUFFAY

400 batów

Les Quatres cen **soups (1959), Polish one sheet**

zdeněk kaplan

(b.1940 Prague, Czechoslovakia)

Between 1964 and 1971, Zdeněk Kaplan worked on just 30 film campaigns yet he is celebrated as one of the most talented and inimitable Czechoslovakian poster artists of the period. Surrealism and wit infused his detail-rich posters. His design for *Le Petit Soldat* is one of his most disturbing works and speaks to the darker themes in Godard's film about the use of torture and the Algerian War.

Kaplan studied at the School of Arts in Prague. He emigrated to America in the late 1960s and then Italy. Of the advertising and film posters he created in Czechoslovakia before this time, some of his most renowned works include *The Seven Year Itch* (1964) *My Fair Lady* (1967) and *End of Desire* (1969).

Anna Karinová ve francouzském filmu režiséra Jean-Luc Godarda

VOJÁČEK

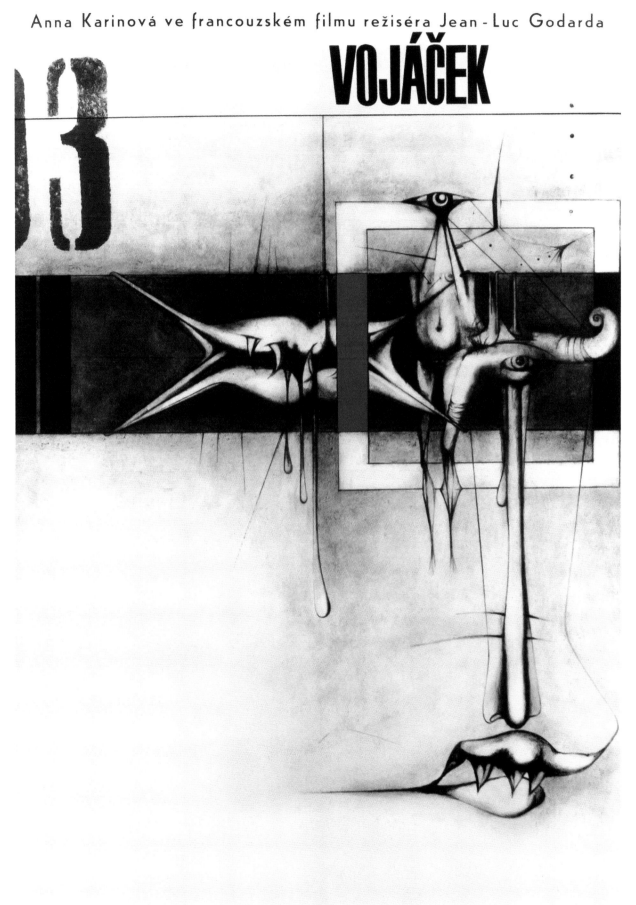

Le Petit Soldat (1960), Czechoslovakian one sheet

zdeněk ziegler

(b.1932, Prague, Czechoslovakia)

A number of posters for *Jules et Jim* were plot-driven or feature a portrait of one or all of the three main leads. Czechoslovakian designer Zdeněk Ziegler was more interested in evoking the atmosphere of the film. By splitting the photograph of Jeanne Moreau and flipping the halves of her face, he emphasises her indecision between Jim and Jules, a fact underscored by the love triangle behind her. The choice of photograph used, with Moreau's enigmatic smile, also manages to capture something of the character's egocentric whimsy.

Ziegler studied at the Czech Technical University, graduating in 1961. He has designed over 300 film, exhibition and theatre posters to date and is one of Czechoslovakia's most celebrated graphic designers. Well-known works include *Psycho* (1960 for first Czech release in 1970), *Midnight Cowboy* (1969 for first Czech release in 1973) and *Raging Bull* (1980 for first Czech release in 1987). He has won several awards for his work and has exhibited at home and abroad. A professor and teacher, he was given an honorary doctorate from Miami University for poster design in 2001, and he was Rector of the Academy of Applied Arts in Prague from 2002 to 2003, where he still lectures today. In 2012, he received the award for Lifelong Contribution to Graphic Design at the 25th Biennale of Graphic Design in Brno.

Jules et Jim (1962), Czechoslovakian one sheet

MADE IN USA

FIN

The five men who killed the groom made one mistake... they should have killed the bride.

additional captions

p.2: Jean-Luc Godard, 1959; p.4 (clockwise from top left): *Paris nous appartient* (1969), still; Claude Chabrol, c.1960s; *À bout de souffle* (1960), still; *Une Femme douce* (1961) French half sheet, art by Chica; *Le Gai savoir* (1969), still; *Model Shop* (1969), American one sheet (detail); *Les Quatres cents coups* (1959), still; Jean-Luc Godard, c.1960s; Claude Jade, 1968; *Chronique d'un été* (1961), French pressbook cover; p.5 *Une Femme est une femme* (1961), still; p.6 (clockwise from top left): *À bout de souffle* (1960), still; *Qui êtes-vous, Polly Maggoo?* (1966), still; *Un Homme et une femme* (1966), still; *La Peau douce* (1964), still; *Pierrot le Fou* (1965), still; *Le Petit Soldat* (1960), still; p.7: *L'Année dernière à Marienbad* (1961), still; p.8: (top) *La Nuit Américaine* (1973), still; (middle) François Truffaut interviewing Alfred Hitchcock, 1962. This interview would form the basis of the authoritative text *Hitchcock/Truffaut* (1966), all photographs © Philippe Halsman/Magnum Photos; (bottom, left to right) first edition of *Cahiers du Cinéma* from April 1951; Claude Chabrol and Jean-Luc Godard in the *Cahiers* offices, 1959; p.12 (clockwise from top left): Director Sam Fuller, c.1950s; *The Searchers* (1956), French one sheet, art by Jean Mascii; *The Big Sleep* (1946), French half sheet, art by Vincent Cristellys; *Pickup on South Street* (1953), French half sheet, art by Constantin Belinsky; p.16 Jean-Pierre Leaud, François Truffaut and Jean Cocteau at the Cannes Film Festival, 1959; p.18-19 Filming the final sequence in *Les Quatres cents coups*, 1959; p.20 (clockwise from top): Jeanne Moreau in *Ascenseur pour l'échafaud* (1958); (right) *Our Man in Paris* album cover (1963), designed by Reid Miles; (left) Jacques Demy and Michel Legrand on the set of *Les Parapluies de Cherbourg* (1964); Michel Legrand at work, c.1960s; *Un Homme et une femme* (1966); Jeanne Moreau and Miles Davis, 1958; p.22 (clockwise from top left): François Truffaut and Françoise Dorléac on the set of *La Peau douce* (1964); Jean-Pierre Melville, c.1960s; Jean-Luc Godard on the set of *Masculin Féminin* (1966); Jean-Luc Godard on the set of *Le Mépris* (1963); Catherine Deneuve and Luis Buñuel on the set of *Belle de Jour* (1967); p.23 (clockwise from top left): Agnès Varda, c.1960s; Delphine Seyrig and Alain Resnais on the set of *L'Année dernière à Marienbad* (1961); Jacques Rivette at a press conference for the release of his controversial film *La Religieuse* (1966); Louis Malle on the set of *Le Feu follet* (1963); François Truffaut, Claire Maurier and Jean-Pierre Leaud at the Cannes Film Festival in 1959; Catherine Deneueve, Nino Castelnuovo and Jacques Demy on the set of *Les Parapluies de Cherbourg* (1964); p.24 (clockwise from top left): *Z*(1969), American one sheet (detail); Harriet Andersson in *Summer with Monika*(1953); *The Man With the Golden Arm* (1955), Design by Saul Bass (detail); *Pierrotle Fou*(1965), still; Brigitte Bardot print with artwork by the British Pop Artist Gerald Laing (1963); *Les Quatre cents coups*(1959), still; *Une Femme mariée*(1964), still; *À bout de souffle*(1960), French tearsheet; p.26 (clockwise from top left): *Ascenseur pour l'échafaud* (1958), French tearsheet; *Moi, un noir* (1958), French one sheet; *Le Petit Soldat* (1960), British quad sheet, art by Peter Strausfeld (detail); *Bande à part* (1964), American lobby card (detail); *Zazie dans le Métro* (1960), French one sheet; *Le Vent d'est* (1970), Italian special sheet; *Les Quatre cents coups* (1959), original Russian artwork; *Le Doulos* (1963), Italian lobby sheet; *Tirez sur le pianiste* (1960), German mini sheet, art by Hans Hillmann (detail); p.27 (clockwise from top left): *Qui êtes-vous, Polly Maggoo?* (1966), French one panel (detail); *Belle de Jour* (1967), Japanese two panel; *À bout de souffle* (1960), American lobby card (detail); *La route de Corinthe* (1967), Italian lobby sheet, art by Renato Ferrini (detail); *Hitler, connais pas* (1963), French medium sheet, *Alphaville* (1965), American one sheet (detail); *Baisers volés* (1968), American one sheet (detail); p.292 (clockwise from top left): *Night and Fog* (1956), Japanese one sheet; *Vivre sa vie*, French mini sheet, art by Vaissier; *Alphaville* (1965), Italian four sheet (detail), art by Averardo Ciriello; *Lola* (1961), French tearsheet; *Pierre et Paul* (1969), Polish one sheet, art by Maciej Hibner; *Deux ou trois choses que je sais d'elle* (1967), French tearsheet (detail); *Les Parapluies de Cherbourg* (1964), Japanese special sheet; p.293 (clockwise from top left): *Made in USA* (1966), French tearsheet (detail); *Une Femme est une femme* (1961), Czechoslovakian one sheet, art by Josef Vyleťal; *Tirez sur le pianiste* (1960), American drive-in sheet, art by M. Koskinen; *La Mariée était en noir* (1968), American one sheet, style B (detail); p.294: Jean-Pierre Leaud in *La Chinoise* (1967); p.297 Jean Seberg in *À bout de souffle* (1960); p.298-299 *Le Mépris* (1963), still; p.303 François Truffaut on the set of *Fahrenheit 451* (1966).

acknowledgements

We would like to thank the following friends and colleagues for their help and support with this Collection over the years: Tarek AbuZayyad; Lisa Baker; Eric Jean-Baptiste; Richard Barclay; Dominique Besson; Robin Boomer; Dave Brolan; Joe Burtis; The Crew from the Island; Christopher Dark; Priya Elan; Leonora Forrester; Leslie Gardner; Armando Giuffrida; Helmut Hamm; Bruce Hershenson; Sarah Hodgson; Andy Howick; Yoshikazu Inoue for his invaluable help in sourcing Japanese artist information; Katsuya Ishida; Andy Johnson; Max Katz; Anne-Marie Kerfyser; John and Billie Kisch; Beth Kleber at School of Visual Arts Archives, New York; Peter Langs; June Marsh; Regina Nepsha; Bill Ndini; Bruno Nouril and Ksenia Yachmetz Nouril; Joakim Olsson; Gabriele Pantucci; Chloe Patmore; Michael Poniz; Eric Rachlis; Walter Reuben; Steve Rose; Janie and Jim Sells; Philip Shalam; Michael Shulman; Dan Strebin; Marta Sylvestrová; Carc   Theakstone; Adam Varkonyi and Carey Wallace.

Special thanks to Serge and Florence Zreik for plar   seed all those years ago;
Kim Goddard and Roxanna Hajiani for helping with th   cataloguing of this collection and the initial artist research;
Daniel Bouteiller for his invaluable help in the research v.   e stills; and John Longhurst

bibliography

Anderson, Joseph L., and Richie, Donald, *The Japanese Film: Art and Industry* (Expanded Edition, Princeton University Press, 1983)

Baroni, Maurizio, *Pittori di Cinema* (Lazy Dog, 2018)

Bryant, Mark 'Obituary: André François', *The Guardian*, 21 April 2005 (<https://www.theguardian.com/obituaries>), accessed 9 June 2019

Capitaine, Jean-Louis, *Ferracci: Affichiste de Cinema* (Albin Michel, 1990)

Cesselon, Alessandra, *The cinema posters of Angelo Cesselon* (<https://youtube.com>), accessed 11 June 2019

Choko, Stanislas, *100 ans d'affiches de cinéma: Description et cote de 20000 affiches* (Les Editions de l'Amateur, 1995)

Culture.pl, *Jan Młodożeniec* (<https://culture.pl>), accessed 25 August 2019

Curry, Adrian, '"The Human Bullet" and the Posters of the Art Theater Guild', *Notebook* (<http://mubi.com/notebook>), accessed 18 August 2019

Curry, Adrian, '"Jules et Jim" and an Interview with Designer Christian Broutin', *Notebook* (<http://mubi.com/notebook>), accessed 4 March 2019

Domenig, Roland, 'The Anticipation of Freedom: Art Theatre Guild and Japanese Independent Cinema', *MidnightEye* (<http://midnighteye.com>), accessed 20 August 2019

Dydo, Krzysztof, *Polish Film Poster: 100th Anniversary of the Cinema in Poland, 1896-1996* (Galeria Plakatu, 1996)

Gid, Raymond, *Typographies* (Imprimerie nationale Éditions, 1998)

Grandt, Jørgen, *Tegneren Aage Lundvald* (<https://grandts.dk>), accessed July 17 2019

Gray, Allan, 'An Investigation of the Precursors to the Nouvelle Vague From Renoir to Resnais 1939-59', *Allan Gray's Imagination* (<https://allangraysimagination.wordpress.com>), accessed 4 April 2019

Gray, Frank 'Peter Strausfeld', *Arts and Culture: University of Brighton* (<http://arts.brighton.ac.uk/alumni-arts/strausfeld,-peter>), accessed 13 September 2019

Gronsky, Libor, Perútka, Marek and Soukup, Michal, *Flashback: Czech and Slovak Film Posters 1959–1989* (Muzeum Umeni Olomouc, 2004)

Guistino, Cathleen M., 'Industrial Design and the Czechoslovak Pavilion at EXPO '58: Artistic Autonomy, Party Control and Cold War Common Ground' *Journal of Contemporary History*, Vol. 47, No. 1 (2012)

Keys, Wendy (director), *Milton Glaser: To Inform and Delight* (2008, available Amazon Prime Video)

Kline, T. Jefferson, *Screening the Text: Intertextuality in New Wave French Cinema* (Johns Hopkins University Press, 2003)

Le Jan, Anne-Laure, 'Une exposition en hommage à Michel Audiard est visible à la médiathèque jusqu'au 12 décembre', *La République du Centre* (<https://larep.fr>, accessed 30 July 2019

Masuda, Miki, 'The Dawn of Art Films in Japan, Art Theatre Guild (ATG): Ushering in Innovative Forms', *Makino Collection Blog* (Columbia University Libraries, 2015) (<https://blogs.cul.columbia.edu>), accessed 23 February 2019

Nemoto, Ryūichirō, *Hisamitsu Noguchi, 1909-1994* (Kaihatsu-sha, 2014)

Nourmand, Tony, *100 Movie Posters: The Essential Collection* (Reel Art Press, 2013)

Ong, Amandas, 'Hans Hillmann: Paper Cinematics', *Elephant* magazine, Issue 16, Autumn 2013

Rabasova Galerie Rakovník, *Josef Hvozdenský* (<https://rabasgallery.cz>), accessed 5 March 2019

Rohmer, Eric, Godard, Jean-Luc, Doniol-Valcroze, Jacques, Domarchi, Jean, Kast, Pierre; Rivette, Jacques 'Hiroshima, Mon Amour: A Round-table discussion', *Cahiers du Cinéma*, July 1959: 13-23. (Reprinted by the Criterion Collection 2003)

Rosen, Miss, 'Graphic Design Icon Milton Glaser on his Legendary Posters', *AnOther* magazine, 19 March 2018 (<https://anothermag.com>), accessed 1 September 2019

Stinson, Liz, 'Milton Glaser on 5 Posters That Taught Him Something About Design', *Aiga Eye on Design* (<https://eyeondesign.aiga.org>), accessed 1 September 2019

Sylvestrová, Marta, *Czech Film Posters of the 20th Century* (Moravian Gallery in Brno and Exlibris Prague, 2004)

Truffaut, François, *The Films in My Life* (Simon and Schuster, 1975, translated by Leonard Mayhew 1978)

Varkonyi, Adam, *'Encyclopedia' of Hungarian Poster Artists*, Budapest Poster Gallery (<https://budapestposter.com>), an invaluable resource on Hungarian poster artists, accessed on several occasions between June and September 2019

'Willy Mucha', *Agnes Thiebault Modern and Contemporary Art* (<https://agnesthiebault.com>), accessed 29 August 2019

Zreik, Serge, *Les Affiches de la Nouvelle Vague 1958-1969* (Éditions du Pécari, 1998)

poster glossary

American

one sheet	41 x 27 in. (104 x 69 cm)
special sheet	sizes vary

Argentinian

one sheet	42 x 28 in. (107 x 72 cm)

British

quad sheet	30 x 40 in. (76 x 102 cm)
special sheet	sizes vary

Czechoslovakian

one sheet	33 x 23 in. (84 x 58 cm)

Danish

one sheet	33 x 24 in (84 x 61 cm)

French

one sheet	63 x 47 in. (160 x 119 cm)
half sheet	31 x 24 in. (79 x 61 cm)
mini sheet	16 x 12 in. (41 x 30 cm)
tear sheet	magazine advertisments

German

one sheet	33 x 23 in. (84 x 58 cm)

Hungarian

one sheet	33 x 22 in. (84 x 55 cm)

Italian

four sheet	79 x 55 in. (201 x 140 cm)
two sheet	55 x 39 in. (140 x 99 cm)
lobby sheet	28 x 13 in (71 x 33 cm)

Japanese

one sheet	28 x 20 in (71 x 51 cm)
two sheet	58 x 20 In (147 x 51 cm)

Polish

one sheet	33 x 23 in. (84 x 58 cm)

*All posters in this book are from the original year of release in their respective countries

poster index

by artist, title and director

photographers index

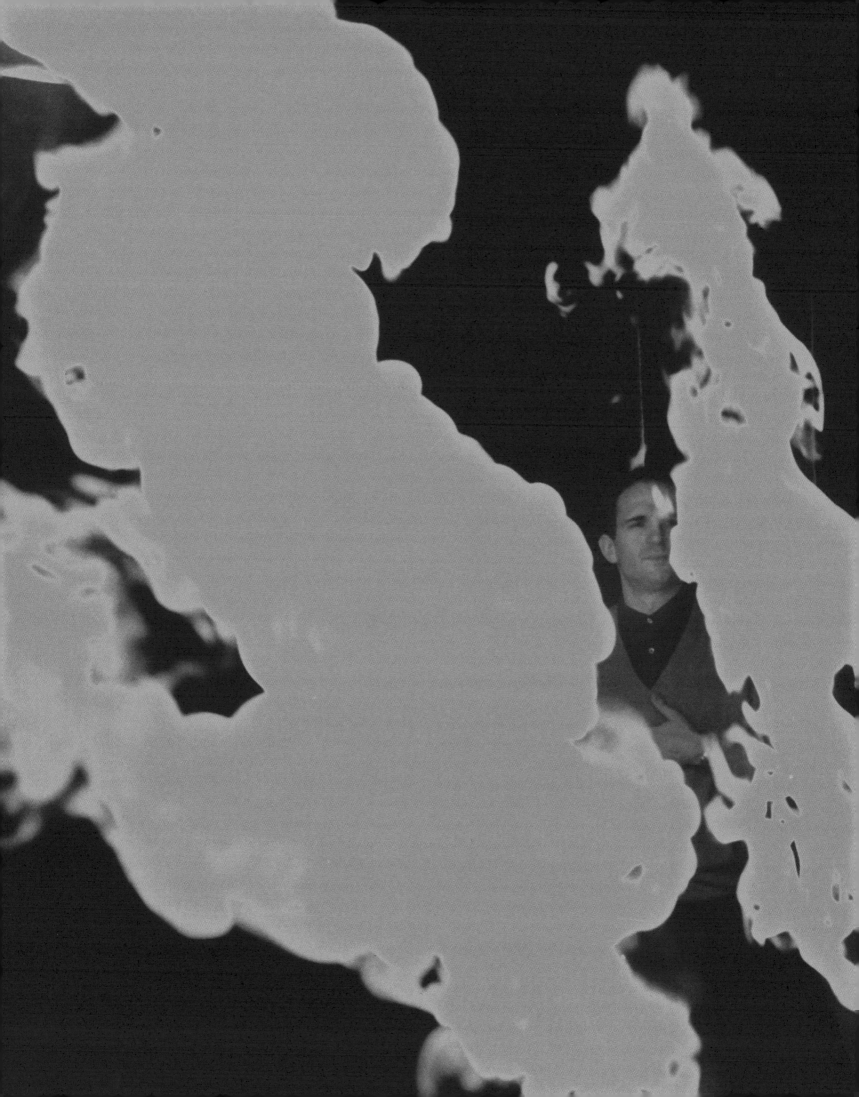

Photography by AJ Photographics
Pre-Press by HR Digital Solutions

First published 2019 by Reel Art Press, an imprint of Rare Art Press Ltd., London, UK

www.reelartpress.com

First Edition
10 9 8 7 6 5 4 3 2 1

ISBN: 978-0-9572610-4-4

All images are reproduced courtesy of The French New Wave Collection (frenchnewwavecollection.com) except:

p.8 middle row (all) © Philippe Halsman/Magnum Photos; p.8 (bottom left): Samuel Aranda/AFP/Getty Images; p.8 (bottom right): Jack Garofalo/Paris Match via Getty Images; p.12 (top and bottom right): Hershenson/Allen Archive; p.22 (bottom right): Jean-Louis Swiners/Gamma-Rapho via Getty Images; p.23 (middle right): Alamy; p.24 (bottom right): © Gerald Laing Art Foundation; p.38 Giancarlo Botti/Gamma-Rapho via Getty Images; p.72& p.82 MPTVimages.net; p.96 Polifilm/Anouchka/Ccc Filmkunst/Kobal/Shutterstock; p.208 Lux Film/Kobal/Shutterstock; p.218 Photofest; p.228 Slon/ Kobal/Shutterstock; p.238 Alinari Archives, Florence/Alinari via Getty Images

The French New Wave Collection is the world's most comprehensive archive of original material advertising the French New Wave.
The Collection features over 3000 items, including original posters from over 20 countries, photographic stills, pressbooks, negatives and more.

Copyright © introduction text: Christopher Frayling
Copyright © *Paris Blues* text: Graham Marsh
Copyright © *La Nouvelle Pop* text: Tony Nourmand
Copyright © Artist biographies text: Alison Elangasinghe

Printed by Graphius, Gent

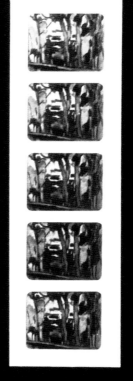

Paris

choisi

Dieu a

e de famille ? Alain retrouvera-t-il un nouveau bonheur auprès

de Dorothy, cette jeune américaine épousée à New-York et qu

a quitté ? Pourrait-il renouer avec ses complices des dernier

jours, futiles, mondains, snobs, intoxiqués ou mythomanes, don

la vie et les délires lui paraissent aujourd'hui dérisoires

Au terme de ces interrogations et de ce pélérinage